SIGILL : COLL : CARLETON
DECLARATIO SERMONUM TUORUM ILLUMINAT
NORTHFIELD, MINN. A.D. 1866

LIBRARY

Gift of

The Bush
Foundation

In Memory Of

Kazuko Nishimoto Fukuhara '62

Dedicated by the
Carleton College
Alumni Association

Literary Lives

General Editor: Richard Dutton, Professor of English, Lancaster University

This series offers stimulating accounts of the literary careers of the most admired and influential English-language authors. Volumes follow the outline of the writers' working lives, not in the spirit of traditional biography, but aiming to trace the professional, publishing and social contexts which shaped their writing.

Published titles include:

Literary Lives
Series Standing Order ISBN 0--333--71486--5 hardcover
Series Standing Order ISBN 0--333--80334--5 paperback
(outside North America only)

You can receive future titles in this series as they are published by placing a standing order. Please contact your bookseller or, in case of difficulty, write to us at the address below with your name and address, the title of the series and one of the ISBNs quoted above.

Customer Services Department, Macmillan Distribution Ltd, Houndmills, Basingstoke, Hampshire RG21 6XS, England

George Herbert

A Literary Life

Cristina Malcolmson
Bates College

First published 2004 by
PALGRAVE MACMILLAN
Houndmills, Basingstoke, Hampshire RG21 6XS and
175 Fifth Avenue, New York, N. Y. 10010
Companies and representatives throughout the world

PALGRAVE MACMILLAN is the global academic imprint of the Palgrave Macmillan division of St. Martin's Press, LLC and of Palgrave Macmillan Ltd. Macmillan® is a registered trademark in the United States, United Kingdom and other countries. Palgrave is a registered trademark in the European Union and other countries.

ISBN 0–333–66978–9 hardback
ISBN 0–333–66979–7 paperback

This book is printed on paper suitable for recycling and made from fully managed and sustained forest sources.

A catalogue record for this book is available from the British Library.

Library of Congress Cataloging-in-Publication Data

Malcolmson, Cristina.
    George Herbert: a literary life / Cristina Malcolmson.
        p. cm. – (Literary lives)
    Includes bibliographical references and index.
    ISBN 0–333–66978–9 – ISBN 0–333–66979–7 (pbk.)
        1. Herbert, George, 1593–1633. 2. Poets, English–Early modern,
1500–1700–Biography. 3. Church of England–England–Clergy–Biography.
I. Title. II. Literary lives (Palgrave Macmillan (Firm))

PR3508.M288 2003
821'.3–dc21
[B]
                                                                    2003054873

10   9   8   7   6   5   4   3
13   12   11   10   09   08   07   06   05

Printed and bound in Great Britain by
Antony Rowe Ltd, Chippenham and Eastbourne

For Jancy and Stan

Contents

Preface

The traditional image of George Herbert as an isolated genius living in retreat from the world has almost completely given way before evidence that the religious poet was publicly engaged, active within an important social circle, and directly concerned with the future of world Protestantism. Nevertheless, exactly what happened in George Herbert's literary career is a mystery that may never be solved. It remains unclear why he begins his professional life as Public Orator at Cambridge, and ends it as a rural minister in Wilton. His major work *The Temple* is similarly enigmatic. Do the devotional lyrics at the center of the work display Herbert's decision to embrace the contemplative life? Or do the long poems at the beginning and end of the work testify to a man engaged in social dynamics and the political problems of the church? The outlines of Herbert's literary career depend entirely on one's perspective on the issue. In this volume, I will follow recent studies that replace an "otherworldly" Herbert with a poet writing public verse, committed to nationalistic Protestantism, and perhaps seeking promotion to higher office until the end of his life.

From this perspective, Herbert's literary career was similar to that of other upper-class men in seventeenth-century England: he wrote to state his views, but also to make his abilities visible for potential patrons. As a younger son in a gentry family, Herbert inherited no land or title, and therefore he had to make a living in order to achieve social independence. But Herbert's upper-class status also determined that he could not write for money without tainting his reputation. Therefore the role of professional writer, which Shakespeare accepted and Ben Jonson embraced, was not an option for Herbert. His literary career was subordinated to the pursuit of public office, whether in church or state. His writing was associated with the institutions and circles he inhabited: the upper-class coterie, Cambridge University, the Church of England.

He was also a poet of the finest ability. His training in rhetoric was intended to prepare him for his work as Reader and Public Orator at Cambridge, and later as an official in the court or church. But there is no doubt that this training came to fruition in his devotional lyrics. Therefore the analysis of the contexts for his writing will include close analysis of the verse. However I will argue that this poetic talent was not developed in individualistic separation from society, but through coterie engagement with other gifted poets of his time: William Shakespeare, John Donne, Mary Sidney Herbert, Mary Wroth, and the less well known William Herbert, Edward Herbert, Benjamin Rudyerd.

George Herbert was the seventh of ten children born to Richard Herbert, Esquire, and Magdalene Herbert, living on the family estate in Montgomery Castle in Wales. After his father died when George was 3, his mother moved the family to Oxford, and later to London. From the outset, Magdalene Herbert had the interests of her sons in mind as she oversaw the career of Edward, her eldest, in Oxford, and then positioned her other sons to be noticed by the London elite. George attended the best preparatory school for classical studies, Westminster School in London (1605–8), went on to Trinity College, Cambridge (1609), and eventually benefited from the patronage of his aristocratic relative, William Herbert, Third Earl of Pembroke. This patronage perhaps extended to support for the position of Public Orator, but almost certainly determined George's seat in Parliament in 1624.[1] Herbert probably had ambitions for public office in mind as early as 1615, since this is the likeliest date for a poem in which John Donne comments that George's destiny included office in the royal court.

However, after Herbert attended Parliament between January and May of 1624, he arranged for a dispensation that granted a hasty ordination into the church after November 3. This is a curious series of events, because ordination made impossible any further participation in the House of Commons, as it put an end to plans for civil employment. Herbert was not, however, ruling out high promotion within the church. Nevertheless, he was not preferred to a full-time post until 1630, and then only to a rural parish. The Earl of Pembroke was again his patron, naming him as rector to the churches of Fulston, outside Wilton Park, and nearby Bemerton. There is evidence as well that he served as chaplain in Wilton House until he died at the age of 40 in 1633.

Scholars speak of Shakespeare's lost years as those when there is no historical record of the playwright. 1625–1630 then are Herbert's mystery years. We have some weak evidence about where he was, but we cannot definitively explain why he never received a position equal to his training, or why he waited five years before he took up work as a minister. Did he turn down more prestigious or more urban positions for the sake of the contemplative life or out of a reluctance to be a priest? Did the illness that plagued him throughout his years make it impossible to accept such positions? Or were no such positions forthcoming, and, if so, why?

Biographies of Herbert offer quite different explanations. Until recently, however, they have by and large characterized Herbert's final years as a retreat from the world. According to Herbert's first biographer, Izaak Walton in 1670, the poet's "court-hopes" died in 1625 with the passing of his major patrons, including King James. F.E. Hutchinson agreed with Walton, and added that Herbert meditated on his unworthiness before he embraced a holy, obscure life in Wiltshire. Amy Charles contended that Herbert planned to join the ministry from the outset, and that his secular ambitions were only a temporary distraction.[2] Building on this foundation, many critics have approached Herbert's lyrics as private meditations. Some scholars have concluded that Herbert's lyrics were kept secret from all until their publication after his death in 1633. This led to a widespread consensus that Herbert withdrew from an antagonistic world, and that his lyrics should be considered private colloquies with his God.[3] These views have prevailed for some time: the usually impressive *Norton Anthology of English Literature* (2000) repeats Walton's chronology, although disproven by Charles, and defines Herbert as "pastor to a small country parish", although he served in the role only for the last three years of his life.[4]

Within the last decade, however, this approach has been radically altered. Some now argue that Herbert never gave up his hopes for prestigious ecclesiastical employment. As Ronald W. Cooley puts it, "The man who wrote *The Country Parson*, then, was a man embarking on a career, not a man who despaired of having one." Michael Schoenfeldt suggests that Herbert never gave up his interest in advancement or his keen powers of courtiership. Jeffrey Powers-Beck and I have provided evidence for the Protestant activism of Herbert's family and a more accurate account of his patronage networks. Recent studies have also provided evidence that Herbert wrote his poetry within the context of coteries, both the upper-class world of Wilton House, and the religious milieu of Little Gidding. His devotional poetry also bears strong resemblance to aspects of the Book of Common Prayer, and therefore may have been conceived as an opportunity for collective worship rather than private meditation. Several critics have demonstrated how thoroughly his lyrics as well as his other writings display his knowledge of contemporary events. No longer imagined as a recluse, George Herbert appears as a man engaged throughout his life with the religion, politics, and society of his time.[5]

The chapters of this book develop an argument about the shape of Herbert's life, as they take up the institutional contexts that influenced his writing. I hope to show that our notions of privacy have distorted Herbert's life and verse, and obscured from view the social and political implications of his religion.

Some clarification is needed about what we know and what we don't know about Herbert's works. Our lack of certainty on these issues has resulted in a great deal of critical debate, particularly in relation to his biography. My intention here is to reproduce the debates when they impinge on the question of Herbert's engagement with society, and, at times, to take a position. For instance, those who presided over the publication of his major works after his death may have added or changed important details. We know that Herbert asked Nicholas Ferrar to publish his collection of poems, but we don't know if Herbert called the work *The Temple*, since the name does not appear in his earliest manuscript, and is written on the copy of the later manuscript in Ferrar's hand.[6] We don't know if Herbert meant "The Church-militant" to be understood as part of the set of poems we call *The Temple*, since "The Church-militant" appears after several empty pages in his earlier manuscript.[7] We don't know if Herbert called his pastoral manual *The Country Parson*, the name given it in 1641 by family members in attempts to get it licensed for publication, or *The Priest to the Temple*, the title at first publication in 1652. This latter issue is especially significant because the royalist, high-church leanings of those publishing the works in 1652 may have obscured Herbert's position on theology and liturgy.[8]

Indeed, the portrait on the cover of this book was drawn long after Herbert's death, in 1670, as a model for the engraving in Izaak Walton's *Lives*.[9] Most critics believe it to be a copy of a lost original portrait, drawn during Herbert's years at Bemerton, but the possibility remains that the asceticism and severity in the face represents Walton's belief in Herbert's retreat from the world far more than it reproduces an accurate likeness of George Herbert. Also, we know that Walton's biography contains a number of inaccuracies and misrepresentations included in order to preach the "gospel of the fitness of the holy life for men of worldly attainment", as David Novarr puts it, whose work, as well as that of Amy Charles, has revealed the problems with Walton's high-church hagiography (see "Suggestions for Further Reading").

Other debates focus on the authorship and dating of particular poems. We can be fairly certain that Herbert wrote everything collected in *The Temple*, as well as *The Country Parson*, but some Cambridge works are not always identified as Herbert's in the manuscripts associated with the University: "To the Lady Elizabeth Queen of Bohemia", "Aethiopissa ambit Cestum Diversi Coloris Virum", and "To the Right Honourable, the Lord Chancellor". Many of the most significant debates include speculation about the dating of undated poems and their relation to the shape of Herbert's life. None of the poems in *The Temple* are dated, but critics frequently speculate about when particular parts were written. For instance, some scholars have dismissed "The Church-porch" and "The Church-militant" as early works, written long before Herbert acquired the asceticism they find in the devotional lyrics. However, others point out that Herbert included these poems in the manuscript intended for publication, whereas he had taken out two Latin collections, *Lucus* and *Passio Discerpta,* from his earlier manuscript. These critics argue that "The Church-porch" and "Church-militant" reflect Herbert's life-long interest in social issues, and that, although they may be less accessible to us, they were equally or perhaps more popular than the lyrics to a seventeenth-century audience. Finally, the two manuscripts of *The Temple* are often described as earlier and later, since "B" includes almost all of the poems in "W" as well as several other poems.[10] This has led to speculation about when Herbert shifted from one manuscript to the other.

Suggestions for further reading

The standard and unsurpassed edition of Herbert's writing, including a remarkable range of information, is *The Works of George*

Herbert, edited by F.E. Hutchinson (first printed 1941, 2nd edition, 1945). The best of the recent editions is *George Herbert: The Complete Poems*, edited by John Tobin (Penguin, 1991). See also *The Latin Poetry of George Herbert: A Bilingual Edition*, edited by Mark McCloskey and Paul R. Murphy (1965), and for Latin poetry and prose, including translations, see *The Complete Works in Verse and Prose*, 3 vols., edited by Alexander Grosart (1874). Very useful is *A Concordance to the Complete Writings of George Herbert*, ed. Mario A. Di Cesare and Rigo Mignani (1977).

The standard biography remains Amy Charles, *A Life of George Herbert* (1977), praiseworthy indeed for its refutations of Walton, although, as usual in Herbert studies, the writer's beliefs about Herbert determine what material is covered. The most egregious example of this is Walton's account of Herbert in *Lives* (1670). This issue is most fully considered by David Novarr in his compelling *The Making of Walton's Lives* (1958) and his "Review: *A Life of George Herbert* by Amy Charles", *George Herbert Journal* 1:2 (1978): 56, 62.

Many recent studies have considered the relationship between Herbert and society, and each makes an argument, at times implicit, about Herbert's biography. These include Leah Marcus, *Childhood and Cultural Despair* (1978), Cristina Malcolmson, *Heart-Work: George Herbert and the Protestant Ethic* (1999), Jeffrey Powers-Beck, *Writing the Flesh: The Herbert Family Dialogue* (1998), Michael Schoenfeldt, *Prayer and Power: George Herbert and Renaissance Courtship* (1991), Debora Shuger, *Habits of Thought in the English Renaissance: Religion, Politics, and the Dominant Culture* (1990); and Marion Singleton, *God's Courtier: Configuring a Different Grace in George Herbert's 'Temple'* (1982). Still remarkably useful on this subject is Joseph Summers, *George Herbert: His Religion and Art* (1968). The collections from the Dearborn conference on seventeenth-century literature and history edited by Claude Summers and Ted-Larry Pebworth offer compelling essays on this issue. *The George Herbert Journal*, edited by Sidney Gottlieb, continues to publish innovative work on all aspects of Herbert studies.

On the subject of locating Herbert within the religious traditions of the seventeenth century, the field is wide, fruitful, and has a very long history. Studies identifying Herbert as a Lutheran or Calvinist in theology include Daniel W. Doerksen, *Conforming to the Word: Herbert, Donne and the English Church Before Laud* (1997); William

Halewood, *The Poetry of Grace* (1970); Christopher Hodgkins, *Authority, Church, and Society in George Herbert: Return to the Middle Way* (1993); Barbara Keifer Lewalski, *Protestant Poetics and the Seventeenth-century Religious Lyric* (1979); Richard Strier, *Love Known: Theology and Experience in George Herbert's Poetry* (1983); and Eugene Veith, *Reformation Spirituality: The Religion of George Herbert* (1985). Chana Bloch demonstrates the centrality of the Bible to Herbert's poetry in *Spelling the Word* (1985). Works that identify Herbert with a more Anglo-Catholic tradition include Louis Martz, *The Poetry of Meditation* (1962); Stanley Stewart, *George Herbert* (1986); Rosemond Tuve, *A Reading of George Herbert* (1952) and R.V. Young, *Doctrine and Devotion in Seventeenth-Century Poetry* (2000). Recent works that challenge this sharp division include Achsah Guibbory, *Ceremony and Community from Herbert to Milton* (1998); Ramie Targoff, *Common Prayer: The Language of Public Devotion in Early Modern England* (2001); and John N. Wall, *Transformations of the Word: Spenser, Herbert, Vaughan* (1988).

There is also a long history of excellent close readings in Herbert criticism. One origin of this tradition is the dispute between William Empson and Rosemond Tuve on the primacy of poetry or theology in the analysis of Herbert's verse (Empson, *Seven Types of Ambiguity*, 1947, 226–33; Tuve, *Reading*). For other valuable examples of close reading, see Stanley Fish, *Self-Consuming Artifacts* (1978); Barbara Harman, *Costly Monuments: Representations of the Self in George Herbert's Poetry* (1982); Mary Ellen Rickey, *Utmost Art: Complexity in the Verse of George Herbert* (1966); Arnold Stein, *George Herbert's Lyrics* (1968); and Helen Vendler, *The Poetry of George Herbert* (1975).[11]

Chronology of Herbert's Life

Contextual Dates

1580 William Herbert born to Henry Herbert, second Earl of Pembroke, and Mary Sidney Herbert, sister to Sir Philip Sidney.

1584 Philip Herbert born, brother to William; perhaps named after Sidney.

1586 Sidney dies.

1588 Benjamin Rudyerd admitted to Inner Temple (admitted to Bar in 1600). Invasion of Spanish Armada fails.

1591 John Donne in Inns of Court until 1596.

1592 Shakespeare first mentioned as playwright in London. Thomas Moffet writes *Nobilis*, the life of Philip Sidney "by way of an example" for William Herbert, commissioned by his mother. William Herbert at New College, Oxford (92–94).

1595 William Herbert first appears in court. Mary Sidney Herbert publishes Philip Sidney's *Apology for Poetry*.

1597 William Herbert in favor with the rival factions of Earl of Essex and Lord Burghley and his son Sir Robert Cecil.

1598 Mary Sidney Herbert publishes Sidney's works.

1599 Queen Elizabeth writes of William Herbert's "good beginnings" to father. Mary Sidney Herbert completes translation of the Psalms left unfinished by her brother. Globe Theater opens.

1600 The anthology *England's Helicon* published (reprinted 1614).

1601	Family moves to Charing Cross, London.
c.1605	Enters Westminster School. Jun. 29 – elected scholar.
1607	John Donne writes to Magdalene Herbert.
c.1608–09	Donne writes poems to Magdalene Herbert, including "these hymns", probably *La Corona*.
1609	Feb. 26 – Mother marries John Danvers. Mar. 5 – Danvers knighted. May – Enters Trinity College, Cambridge as King's scholar. Dec. 18 – matriculates as pensioner at Trinity.

1601 William Herbert becomes Earl of Pembroke. Essex rebellion; John Danvers' brother Charles executed for his part in the rebellion. John Donne secretly marries Anne More.

1602 *Poetical Rhapsody* published (including Hoskyns' "Absence") dedicated by Francis Davison to Pembroke.

1603 Mar. 24 – Death of Queen Elizabeth; accession of James I. King creates numerous new knights; inflation of honors and increased spending begins.

1604 King makes peace with Spain. At Hampton Court conference, king rejects Puritan Millenary Petition requesting changes in ceremony. Anti-Puritan Richard Bancroft named Archbishop of Canterbury. King claims that Parliament holds its privileges only through him. Parliament, 1604–1610.

1605 Gunpowder Plot by extremist Catholics fails to blow up Parliament and the royal family. Philip Herbert, William's brother, becomes a favorite to the king; Philip named Earl of Montgomery.

1606 King James gives Montgomery Castle to Philip Herbert. Charters given to the London and Plymouth Companies to colonize Virginia.

1607 Robert Carr becomes royal favorite. Virginia settled by Captain John Smith. Sep. 14 – Plantation of Ulster

1608 The Protestant Union, including the Palatine, forms in Germany as part of the Holy Roman Empire to defend itself against the Catholic majority. The Palatine Council votes to seek a marriage between Prince Frederick and Princess Elizabeth, daughter of James I. "State-Progress of Ill" by Edward Herbert, George's brother, answers Donne's "The Progress of the Soul" (1601).

1609 Feb. – John Donne applies for secretaryship in Virginia Company; eventually his bid is unsuccessful. May 23 – Pembroke becomes member of the king's council for the Virginia Co. Shakespeare's sonnets published apparently without his approval.

1610	Jan. 1 – Gives mother New Year's sonnets with letter.
1612	After Nov. 6 – poems on the death of Prince Henry published in Cambridge volume.
1613	Feb. 17 – Bachelor of Arts. Late Feb. – Frederick, Elector Palatine and husband to Princess Elizabeth, visits Cambridge with Prince Charles. Herbert contributes two poems to the commemorative volume presented to Frederick.
1614	Minor fellow, Trinity.

1610   Sep. – News of survival of the Virginia expedition reaches London. Calvinist George Abbot appointed Archbishop of Canterbury. Donne responds to "State-Progress of Ill" by Edward Herbert in a verse letter. Edward Herbert fights for the Protestant Union at Juliers.

1611   Anglo-Palatine marriage arranged; James I makes six-year alliance with the Protestant Union for defense against Catholic attack. King James Bible published. Pembroke becomes privy councilor. Fall – *Tempest* produced at court.

1612   Death of king's secretary Robert Cecil, Earl of Salisbury; power of the royal favorite Robert Carr increases. Jul. 26 – Pembroke an incorporator of the North-West Passage Company. Nov. 6 – Protestant Prince Henry dies. John Danvers becomes member of the Virginia Co.

1612–13 Ben Jonson collects his epigrams, dedicated to Pembroke, including verses to Benjamin Rudyerd, Mary Wroth, Edward Herbert, John Donne, Thomas Overbury.

1613   Feb. 14 – Wedding of Princess Elizabeth to German Protestant Frederick, Elector Palatine; *Tempest* produced at court in preceding festivities. John Donne and Edward Herbert publish poems on the death of Prince Henry in a volume edited by Josuah Sylvester. Apr. – Donne visits Edward Herbert in Montgomery. Jul. – Philip Herbert gives Montgomery Castle back to Edward Herbert for L500. Royal favorite Robert Carr marries Frances Howard after she obtains a divorce from her husband, opposed by Archbishop Abbot. Thomas Overbury poisoned in the Tower of London.

1614   Addled Parliament. Privy Councilor and Attorney General Francis Bacon excluded from House of Commons. James I refuses military support for Protestant Union at Julich, but settles the dispute through mediation. Plans for Spanish marriage begin; James increasingly influenced by the Spanish ambassador, Gondomar. Edward Herbert fights for Protestant Union under the Prince of Orange; visits the Elector Palatine and Queen Elizabeth in Heidelberg. Pembroke becomes a life-long member of the East India Company.

1615	Jan. 23 – Donne ordained; most likely period for Donne's Latin poem to Herbert.
1616	Mar. 15 – Major fellow, Trinity; Master of Arts.
1617	Oct. 2 – Sublector (lecturer), Trinity. Brothers William and Charles probably died this year.
1618	Jan. 1 – Writes the University letter to Buckingham on his becoming Marquis. Three letters to Sir John Danvers, including one requesting money for books for "setting foot into Divinity" (Mar. 18). Jun. 11 – Praelector in rhetoric, Cambridge. Dec. 26 – Letter of gossip and court news written for Sir John Danvers to Sir Robert Harley. Most likely year for letter of advice to brother Henry.
1619	After Mar. 2 – Poem on the death of Queen Anne published in Cambridge volume. Sep. – Letter to Danvers requesting help in obtaining Public Oratorship, and sending through him a similar request to Sir Francis Nethersole. Oct. 6 – Letter to Danvers reassuring him and Nethersole that the Oratorship will not interfere with ordination; also speaks of visiting his sister Elizabeth, Lady Johnes, 200 miles away. Oct. 21 – Appointed deputy Orator, Cambridge. Most likely year for official letter to Bishop Lancelot Andrewes.

1615   Jan. 23 – Donne ordained as deacon and priest. Feb. – Donne appointed royal chaplain. Mar. – Donne given honorary degree as Doctor of Divinity at Cambridge by royal mandate. Jun. 29 – Pembroke an incorporator for the Bermudas Company. Frances Howard and Robert Carr tried for the murder of Thomas Overbury, convicted and pardoned by King. Dec. – Buckingham replaces Robert Carr as royal favorite; Pembroke becomes lord chamberlain.

1616   Shakespeare dies. Ben Jonson's *Works* published. Edward Herbert again visits Frederick and Elizabeth in Heidelberg. John Smith, *A Description of New England.*

1617   Jan. – Dean of Gloucester William Laud places the communion table altar-wise at the east end of the Cathedral. Mid-year: Francis Burgoyne does the same in Durham Cathedral, probably for Bishop Richard Neile. Jan. 29 – Pembroke becomes Chancellor of Oxford. Buckingham becomes earl.

1618   Thirty Years' War begins: May 23 – Bohemians rebel against their Catholic rulers; potential for Protestant majority among Electors for Holy Roman Empire in Germany. Nov. 13 – May 9, 1619 – With support from James I, the Synod of Dort opposes Arminianism by affirming principles of predestinarian Calvinism; John Davenant a delegate. Benjamin Rudyerd knighted. Book of Sports issued.

1619   May 13 – Edward Herbert leaves for Paris as ambassador to France, named by Buckingham. Nicholas Ferrar becomes member of Virginia Co. Donne preaches before Frederick, Elector Palatine, and Queen Elizabeth in Heidelberg. Aug. 22 – Bohemia deposes Hapsburg Archduke Ferdinand, offers crown to Frederick. Aug. 28 – Imperial Electors choose Ferdinand as Holy Roman Emperor. Sep. 19 – Francis Nethersole appointed English secretary to Elizabeth, Electress Palatine. Sep. 28 – Frederick accepts Bohemian crown against King James' advice. Autumn – James shows his disapproval for Frederick's act; offers to mediate; sends ambassadors not money or troops so as not to interfere with plans to marry Prince Charles to the Spanish princess.

1620	Jan. 19 – Letter to Danvers requesting news of his oldest sister Elizabeth and her son, perhaps Herbert's godson; notes that the Orator election is soon. Jan. 21 – Elected Public Orator, Cambridge. May 20 – Writes official letter of thanks to King James on the gift of his *Opera Latina* to Cambridge. Jun. 14 – Writes official letters of thanks to King James; Robert Naunton, secretary of state; Francis Bacon, Lord Chancellor; and Fulke Greville for their help in prohibiting the draining of the Bedford fens. Oct. 14 – Bacon gives *Instauratio Magna* to Cambridge. Nov. 4 – Writes official letter of thanks to Francis Bacon for the gift of *Instauratio Magna* to Cambridge. Writes two Latin poems in honor of Bacon's work. Dec. 20 – Writes letter "For my dear sick Sister," Elizabeth.
c.1620–21	*Musae Responsoriae*, dedicated to King James, Prince Charles, and Bishop Lancelot Andrewes.
c.1621–22	Probable author of "To the Lady Elizabeth Queen of Bohemia", most likely written in these years.
1621	Jan. 29 – writes official letters to Archbishop George Abbot and Francis Bacon on the Cambridge printers. Between Jan. 27 and May 1 – writes most famous Latin poem to Bacon. Oct. 8 – writes official letter to Lionel Cranfield, Treasurer.
1622	May 29 – Writes letter to mother in her sickness. Dec. 15 – Edward Herbert dedicates his manuscript of *De Veritate* to George and William Boswell, and asks that they edit out anything contrary to good morals and religion.

1620   Autumn – Spanish invade Palatinate; James promises his support for its restoration to Frederick. Oct. 14 – Francis Bacon publishes *Novum Organon*, the second part of *The Great Instauration*. Nov. – Bohemia lost to Catholic forces. Nov. 3 – Pembroke named to council for New England; patents 30,000 acres in Virginia, and undertakes to send over emigrants and cattle. Pilgrims land at Plymouth.

1621   Jan. 27 – Francis Bacon created Viscount St. Albans. Apr. – Frederick and Elizabeth in Holland. Denmark and Dutch Republic make support for Frederick dependant on aid from England. James seeks to protect the Palatinate through mediation and Spanish marriage; dissolves Parliament in Dec. for advocating war with Spain. Sir Edwin Sandys, administrator of the Virginia Company, gains power in Parliament. Benjamin Rudyerd makes his first appearance in the Commons. May 1 – Chancellor Francis Bacon impeached for corruption by House of Commons over royal monopolies; Pembroke defends Bacon. Sep. – Death of Mary Sidney Herbert. Donne writes verses on the translation of the Psalms by Mary and her brother Philip Sidney. Nov. 22 – Donne becomes dean of St. Paul's. Mary Wroth's *Urania* published. John Davenant named Bishop of Salisbury.

1622   Mar. – Pembroke introduces Henry Herbert, George's brother, to King James; Henry becomes the King's servant. Jul. 3 – Donne chosen honorary member of Virginia Co. Aug. – King's "Directions on Preachings" forbids to all but bishops and deans references in sermons to predestination and Rome. Nov. 3 – Donne preaches sermon to Virginia Company; sermon published. Dec. 15 – Edward Herbert dedicates his manuscript of *De Veritate* to his secretary William Boswell and George Herbert. Richard Herbert dies at the siege of Bergen-op-Zoom.

1623   Feb. 27 – Delivers oration to Spanish and the Austrian
              ambassadors awarded honorary Masters of Arts. Mar. 12
              – Gives short speech of farewell and epigram to King
              James as he leaves Cambridge. Epigram appreciated by
              Arminians John Richardson and Bishop Richard Neile.
              Epigram and oration of Feb. 27 published that year
              "by command." Aug. 14 – Sister Margaret buried. After
              Aug. 23, *Lucus* and *Passio Discerpta*. Oct. 8 – Delivers
              anti-war speech to Prince Charles and Duke of
              Buckingham; oration published that year. Dec. – Named
              to Parliament for Montgomery borough under purview
              of the Earl of Pembroke. Translates Bacon's *Advancement
              of Learning* into Latin for *De Augmentis Scientiae*.

1624   Feb. through May – Member of Parliament. Serves on
              committee hearing charges against masters of colleges
              or schoolmasters. Committee drops unspecified charges
              against the Master of Trinity, John Richardson. Jun. 11
              – Granted six-month leave from Orator's duties by
              Cambridge. Nov. 3 – Dispensation by Archbishop
              Abbot for immediate ordination as a deacon rather
              than after the usual year of probation, and through
              Bishop John Williams. Dec. 6 – Granted sinecure in
              Montgomeryshire by Bishop Williams. Dec. 11 – six-
              month leave from Cambridge ends.

1623   Shakespeare's First Folio published and dedicated to William and Philip Herbert. Feb. – Electors replace Frederick with Catholic Maximilian of Bavaria as Elector Palatine; Frederick plans a new assault. Prince Charles and Buckingham travel to Spain. May – Buckingham becomes duke. Aug. – King knights Henry Herbert; names him Master of the Revels. Aug. 6 – Palatinate decisively lost in battle of Stadtlohn. Oct. 5 – After finding the conditions for the Spanish marriage unacceptable, Charles and Buckingham return from Spain in a ship captained by Thomas Herbert, George's brother. Charles makes the restoration of the Palatinate a precondition for the Spanish marriage. Late in the year – Andrewes, Laud, Neile, and Prince Charles' chaplain Matthew Wren confer on the prince's receptivity to Arminianism.

1624   Buckingham and Prince Charles support war with Spain; Pembroke votes against them in the privy council in January, but later supports them. Feb.–May – parliament votes for war. Buckingham begins negotiations for marriage between Charles and the Catholic French princess, Henrietta Maria. Arminian Richard Montagu claims predestination is no part of Thirty-Nine Articles; parliamentary attacks on Arminianism begin. Apr. – Edward Herbert dismissed as ambassador to France; publishes *De Veritate* in Paris. Jun. – Virginia Company supported by Ferrar, Danvers, and Pembroke dissolved by order of King James; Danvers or Ferrar has records copied; Virginia becomes a royal province. Henry Herbert reprimanded for licensing Middleton's *A Game at Chesse*. Sep. – Buckingham excludes Pembroke from marriage negotiations with the French. Edward Herbert named to king's council of war and, in December, admitted to Irish peerage with inconsequential title of Lord Herbert of Castle Island. Dec. – Laud draws up for Buckingham a tract that defines Calvinism as Puritanism. Buckingham prevents Pembroke from becoming a duke and signing the marriage treaty with the French.

1625   May 7 – Herbert's deputy gives the oration at
            Cambridge's commemoration of the death of King
            James. Herbert contributes no verses to university col-
            lections on James' death and Charles' marriage.
            Ineligible for parliament May–August. Walton claims
            that Herbert is in "retirement" staying with a "Friend
            in *Kent*". Dec. 21 – Donne, escaping the plague by
            staying at Sir John Danvers's house in Chelsea from
            July, writes to Goodyer that "Mr. *George Herbert* is
            here." Bacon dedicates his *Translation of Certaine
            Psalmes into English Verse* to "his very good frend
            Mr. George Herbert."

1626   After Apr. 9 – Latin poem published in Cambridge
            volume in memory of Bacon; Herbert may have col-
            lected contributors. Jul. 5 – Installed by proxy as canon
            of Lincoln Cathedral and prebendary of Leighton
            Ecclesia through patronage of Bishop John Williams;
            yearly sermon his only duty. Jul. 13 – Delivers oration
            in York House at the installation of Buckingham as
            Chancellor of Cambridge. Probably visits Leighton
            Bromswold (near Little Gidding) at some point for
            actual installment. Lives with brother Henry at
            Woodford, Essex, as he recovers from illness, through
            use of diet, according to Walton, as corrected by
            Leishman (xxxiii).

1625   Henry Herbert marries Susan Plomer, widow of a merchant
        taylor; acquires houses in Woodford and Kilbourn in Essex.
        Mar. 2 – Marquis of Hamilton dies. Mar. 27 – King James
        dies; Laud draws up for the new king a list of leading
        clergy considered "orthodox" (Arminian) and "puritan"
        (Calvinist). Mar. – England at war with Spain (to 1630).
        Jun.–Aug. – in parliament, Charles intervenes in support of
        Arminian Robert Montagu; Commons begins investigation
        of Buckingham perhaps supported by Pembroke; king
        dissolves session. Aug. – plague begins in London. Sep. –
        Thomas Herbert named by Buckingham as captain to the
        Dreadnought on expedition with Dutch to Cadiz. Oct. –
        John Williams dismissed as Lord Keeper perhaps as
        warning to Pembroke. Dec. – Cadiz expedition fails. Dec. 9
        – Hague convention includes promise of England and
        Dutch Republic to fund Christian IV of Denmark, who
        becomes leader of Protestant forces against the Catholic
        Hapsburgs.

1626   Feb. – York House Conference on Calvinism vs.
        Arminianism; Buckingham supports Arminians. Apr. 9 –
        Bacon dies. Feb.–Jun. – Henry Herbert serves in parliament
        in same seat formerly held by George. Pembroke's clients
        support impeachment attempts against Buckingham. Jun.
        4 – Nicholas Ferrar ordained deacon by Laud; retires with
        family to Little Gidding. Jun. 14 – Royal proclamation bans
        Calvinism from press and pulpit. Jun. 15 – king dissolves
        parliament. Jun. 16 – Calvinist sermon planned for
        Cambridge commencement stopped by king. Jul. –
        Pembroke and Buckingham reconciled through marriage
        planned between Pembroke's heir, Montgomery's son, and
        Buckingham's daughter. Jul. 13 – Buckingham installed as
        Chancellor of Cambridge University; Buckingham silences
        Calvinism at Cambridge. Pembroke keeps it alive at
        Oxford. Aug. 18 – Pembroke becomes lord steward;
        Montgomery lord chamberlain. Aug. 26 – Count Tilly
        defeats the Protestant army of Christian IV of Denmark at
        Lutter. Sep. 25 – Lancelot Andrewes dies. Oct. – Laud
        promised succession to Canterbury. William Prynne, *The
        Perpetuitie of a Regenerate Man's Estate*. The Dutch buy
        Manhattan Island for $24.

1627   May 6 (?) – at Chelsea, writes letter of advice to deputy orator Robert Creighton which signals Herbert's readiness to resign position. Shortly before Jun. 8 – mother dies. Jul. 7 – *Memoriae Matris Sacrum* entered with Donne's funeral sermon at the Stationer's Register. By Jul. 14 – Crown grants manor of Ribbesford to George, Edward, and cousin Thomas Lawley. Henry Herbert buys the manor for L3000.

1628   Jan. 29 – Cambridge Senate names Robert Creighton Public Orator. Herbert living with Earl of Danby, brother to John Danvers, in Dauntesey, near Chippenham, Wiltshire, according to Walton.

1627   Apr. – Arminians Laud and Neile made privy councilors. May – Pembroke an incorporator of the Guiana Company. Summer – The Catholic forces of Tilly and Wallenstein occupy and ravage Jutland in Denmark. Jun. – England at war with France (to 1629). Jun. 27 – Buckingham sails out to support Huguenot rebellion at La Rochelle, and to capture the Isle of Rhê. Nov. – failure of Buckingham's expedition to the Isle of Rhé; the duke asks Edward Herbert to write a defense.

1628   Laud preaches opening sermon before parliament. Commons names Bishops Laud and Neile untrustworthy for their Arminianism. Sir Robert Harley speaks against Arminianism as a threat to national security. Charles agrees to Petition of Right, asserting rule of law over royal perogative. Parliament votes Charles subsidies. Jul. – Laud becomes Bishop of London; begins prosecution of non-conformity. Jul. 10 – John Danvers marries Elizabeth Dauntsey, moves to Lavington, Wiltshire. Aug. 23 – Buckingham assassinated. Oct. 28 – Calvinist Huguenots surrender at La Rochelle; fears of Catholic invasion of England grow. Neile becomes Bishop of Winchester; orders the Cathedral communion table be placed altar-wise. Arminian George Montaigne named Archbishop of York. Calvinism again proscribed through royal decree. Prynne, *A Briefe Survay and Censure of Mr. Cozens his Couzening Devotions*. Henry Burton explains the rise of Arminianism as a Popish plot in *Israel's Fast*. Massachusetts Bay Colony settled by Puritans.

1629	Mar. 5 – marries Jane Danvers, cousin to the Earl of Danby, in Edington Church, Baynton. Couple moves to Baynton House, Wiltshire, with wife's family, according to Walton. According to Aubrey, couple lives with Earl of Danby. May 24 – gives sermon at Lincoln Cathedral. Oct. 29 – Living at Bemerton open after King promotes Walter Curle, rector of Bemerton and Bishop of Rochester, to Bishopric of Bath and Wells.
1630	Apr. 16 – Deed of presentation of Bemerton St. Andrew and Fugglestone St.Peter to Herbert. Apr. 26 – instituted by John Davenant, Bishop of Salisbury; installed at Bemerton. May 16 – Herbert misses first possible date for ordination; according to Charles he preaches instead at Lincoln Cathedral and offers Ferrar prebendary (which Ferrar turns down). May 23 – Nathanael Bostocke, Herbert's curate, ordained. Autumn (?) – letter to brother Henry at court about taking into the Bemerton rectory two nieces, daughters of the second oldest sister, Margaret (d.1623) from Edward Herbert's household; asks Henry to adopt a third; speaks of spending 200 pounds on "building", probably the Bemerton rectory. Sep. 19 – Herbert ordained as priest in Salisbury Cathedral.

1629   Charles calls another session of 1628 parliament. Commons accuses the Crown of labeling all non-Arminians "Puritans" and promoting only Arminian clergy; asks that future bishops be chosen with advice from the Privy Council. Parliament refuses to vote the king funds from Tonnage and Pountage. Feb. – Bishop John Williams preaches in favor of Calvinism before the House of Lords. Mar. 2 – Charles dissolves session; nine members of parliament arrested. Personal Rule begins (to 1640). Apr. 14 – Peace with France. May 7 – Edward Herbert created Lord Herbert of Cherbury. Oct. 11 – King issues proclamation calling for the restoration of churches and chapels. Prynne, *God no Imposter nor Deluder.* Massachusetts Bay Company is formed in England with John Winthrop as Governor. The Council for New England grants New Hampshire to John Mason, and King Charles grants Robert Heath the territory named Carolina.

1630   Edward Herbert dedicates his account of the expedition of the Isle of Rhé to Charles; no royal recognition ensues. Mar. – John Davenant, bishop of Salisbury, gives sermon on predestination at Whitehall; rebuked by king before the Privy Council; according to Prynne, Davenant kept communion table in middle of chancel throughout this period. Apr. 10 – William Herbert dies, mourned as Calvinist leader; Philip Herbert becomes fourth earl of Pembroke. Apr. 12 – Laud elected Chancellor of Oxford defeating Philip Herbert by nine votes. Jun. – Gustavus Adolphus, King of Sweden, becomes leader of Protestant forces in Germany. Charles allows Marquis of Hamilton to levy troops, but gives no more aid. Oct. – Henry Sherfield, town official, breaks stained-glass window in St. Edmund's church, Salisbury; prosecution by Star Chamber initiated by Bishop Davenant; fined L500. Dec. 5 – Peace with Spain, without restoration of Palatinate, but with promises of help. 1630–31 – bad harvest, rise in price of wheat, famine. Prynne, *Anti-Arminianisme or the Church of England's Old Antithesis to New Arminianisme.* John Winthrop and 1,000 Puritans land at Salem, MA, and soon found Boston. Winthrop's reasons include bringing the fullness of the Gentiles into the kingdom of God, and escaping God's judgment coming upon the corrupt churches of Europe ("Reasons for Emigrating to New England").

1631   Oct. – writes up reasons for Arthur Woodnoth to continue in the service of John Danvers. Dec. 10 – letter to Lady Anne, Countess of Pembroke and Montgomery [formerly Anne Clifford] at court.

1632   Mar. 21 – letter to brother Henry at court on rebuilding Leighton church. March – two letters to Nicholas Ferrar on the same. Jun. 7 – short letter to brother Henry asking for news (could be 1631). Aug. 15 – niece Dorothy Vaughan buried at Bemerton. Sep. 29 – returns Ferrar's translation of Valdesso's *Considerations* with Herbert's commendatory letter and "Brief Notes". *Country Parson* dated 1632.

1633   Feb. 25 – dictates will to curate Nathanael Bostocke. Mar. 1 – dies. Mar. 3 – buried in the chancel of St. Andrews Church, Bemerton, without inscription. Mar. 12 – will proved by Arthur Woodnoth. Sep. – *Temple* published at Cambridge through efforts of Nicholas Ferrar, and after delay of Cambridge licenser over lines in "The Church-militant" on religion fleeing from England to America.

1631   Mar. 31 – Donne dies. Oct. – Among many Protestant victories in Germany, Adolphus defeats Tilly's forces. Henry Vane negotiates over Palatinate, but Adolphus unsympathetic. 1631–34 – Isaac de Caus lays out an Italian garden at Wilton House, home of Philip Herbert, fourth earl of Pembroke. Rebellions against enclosure in areas around Bemerton – Warminster, Chippenham, Selwood, Braydon. Oct. – Philip Herbert calls out armed bands to quell rebellion in Warminster. Roger Williams arrives in Boston; Sir Ferdinando Gorges begins settlement of Maine/New Hampshire area.

1632   Edward Herbert named to council of war. Neile becomes Archbishop of York. Summer – Spanish lose Maastricht in Low Countries to Dutch. Jun. – Thomas Roe and Francis Nethersole argue against Spanish peace and for Dutch alliance; Nethersole dismissed from Elizabeth's service through Charles' influence. Nov. – Frederick, Elector Palatine, dies; Gustavus Adophus, King of Sweden, dies. France urges alliance with England to oppose Hapsburgs; restoration of the Palatinate to Frederick's son not clearly a French priority. Work begins on a Catholic chapel in Somerset House for Queen Henrietta Maria. Lord Baltimore granted the Maryland charter by Charles I.

1633   Aug. – George Abbot dies; Laud becomes Archbishop of Canterbury. Oct. – Book of Sports reissued; its enforcement required. Nov. – King calls for the placing of the communion table altar-wise in St. Gregory's Church, adjoining St. Paul's Cathedral; initiates full-fledged Arminian reform. The colony of Maryland settled.

1
The Sidney-Herbert Coterie

When George Herbert composed sonnets for his mother for New Year's Day, 1610, he wrote very soon after the publication of Shakespeare's sonnets in 1609, with the knowledge that his family was related to Sir Philip Sidney, the originator of the English sonnet sequence, and with an awareness of the poetic exchange between his brother Edward Herbert and John Donne. Because George's sonnets announced his intention to write religious lyrics, modern critics have concluded that he defined his poetry in opposition to the secular love celebrated by Sidney, Shakespeare, and Donne. Yet each of these poets also condemned erotic love, and Sidney and Donne argued that sacred love was preferable. George Herbert therefore took his place as perhaps the most adamant but in no way the first in the Sidney-Herbert coterie to advocate religious love as the proper subject for sonnets.

George was a member of the gentry Herberts as well as fourth cousin to the aristocratic Herbert family, which included the earls of Pembroke. In 1577, the second earl married Mary Sidney, Sir Philip Sidney's sister. Mary's child, the third earl, William Herbert (b.1580), was Sidney's nephew, as well as literary patron to Shakespeare, Ben Jonson, Samuel Daniel, William Browne, John Earle, and George Wither. It is significant but rarely noted in studies of George Herbert that Mary Sidney Herbert as Countess of Pembroke presided over Wilton House for the first 10 years of George Herbert's life until her son took over in 1603, and that the Countess of Pembroke published during this time most of Philip Sidney's works, including *Astrophil and Stella* and *The Apology for*

1

Poetry. Therefore the Protestant coteries that the Countess of Pembroke and her son fostered should be considered as having a fundamental influence on George's formation as a poet.

In a recent renewal of scholarly attention, the coterie exchange of poetry has been analyzed as the primary alternative to print publication for the upper classes. These coteries included evenings of entertainment in which poetry was recited or sung with musical accompaniment, as well as the exchange of manuscripts and keeping of commonplace books, in which poems were copied and imitated.[1] The exchange of verses between individuals, whether male or female, testified to an intellectual friendship, but it could also accompany a political alliance or a patron-client relationship. After William became the third earl of Pembroke, he provided patronage to several writers who had formed a coterie within the inns of court.[2] William Herbert formed such a relationship with Benjamin Rudyerd, who later became Herbert's spokesperson in the House of Commons. The poetic exchange between Herbert and Rudyerd was present in manuscripts throughout the period, and published after their death by John Donne's son in 1660 in the volume *Poems Written by the Right Honorable William Earl of Pembroke Lord Steward of his Majesties Houshold. Whereof Many of which are answered by way of Repartee, by Sr Benjamin Ruddier, Knight, with several Distinct Poems, Written by them Occasionally, and Apart*.[3] William's mother, the Countess of Pembroke, established a patronage relationship with her niece Lady Mary Wroth, who broke upperclass rules and published her work *Urania* in 1621, dedicating it to the Countess.[4]

The Herbert-Rudyerd volume highlights a form basic to coterie exchange: the answer-poem. The title refers to this form: *Whereof Many of which are answered by way of Repartee*. In answering, the second writer honors the first by choosing his or her poem for imitation, but also contests with it by offering commentary or outdoing the other through displays of witty invention.[5] The most famous answer-poem is Sir Walter Raleigh's "Nymph's Reply to Her Shepherd", although there were in fact multiple answers throughout this period to Christopher Marlowe's "The Passionate Shepherd to his Love", one of which was in the Herbert-Rudyerd volume.[6] The answer-poem and the wit battle seem to have been particularly emphasized in the festivities of the Inns of Court, where many poets got their start, including John Donne and Benjamin Rudyerd. George Herbert's "sacred parody", in which secular wit is turned to religious purposes, should be seen as a process of answering on a large, even a lifetime scale.[7]

Most of George's answer-poems address verses associated with the Sidney-Herbert coterie. The sonnets to his mother, their later incarnation as "Love" (I) and (II) in *The Temple*, and the "Jordan" poems respond to Sidney's *Astrophil and Stella* and *Apology for Poetry*. "Jordan" (II) refers as well to Shakespeare's sonnets 21 and 129, the former itself an answer to a Sidney poem. Finally, "A Parodie" is George's version of the poems on absence that Sidney initiated in his sonnet sequence, members of the Inns of Court developed at the beginning of the 1600's, and John Donne, Edward Herbert, and William Herbert transformed into the famous topic of "mutual love". William Herbert's "Soule's Joy" is clearly the poem that "A Parodie" answers, but Donne's "Valediction: forbidding Mourning" and Sidney's poems on absence are evoked as well.

The sonnets to his mother and "Love" (I) and (II) advocate sacred purposes for love as well as the dedication of poetic invention to God. Both sets of poems encourage writers to lay "All [their] invention on thine Altar" ("Love" II).[8] The beginnings of the plan for *The Temple* with its opening lyric "The Altar" seems already to be in Herbert's mind in 1610: "Why are not *Sonnets* made of thee? and layes/ Upon thine Altar burnt?" (Sonnet I to his mother, lines 5–6). This plan is conceived in association with Sidney's *Apology* (publ.1595):

> Other sort of poetry almost have we none, but that lyrical kind of songs and sonnets: which, Lord, if He gave us so good minds, how well it might be employed, and with how heavenly fruit, both private and public, in singing the praises of the immortal beauty: the immortal goodness of that God who giveth us hands to write and wits to conceive; of which we might well want words, but never matter; of which we could turn our eyes to nothing, but we should ever have new-budding occasions.

Sidney describes the Psalms as "heavenly poesy wherein almost [David] showeth himself a passionate lover of that unspeakable and everlasting beauty to be seen by the eyes of the mind, only cleared by faith."[9] This preference for spiritual rather than mortal beauty is expressed in *Certain Sonnets* #32 as well:

> Leave me, O love which reachest but to dust,
> And thou, my mind, aspire to higher things;
> Grow rich in that which never taketh rust;
> What ever fades, but fading pleasure brings ...
>   Then farewell, world; thy uttermost I see;
>   Eternal love, maintain thy life in me. (1–4, 13–14)

Sidney's poem uses the same terms as his comments in the *Apology*: God created the eyes of man to perceive immortal beauty rather than the fading impostures of physical loveliness. So God also created the mind of man to be nourished by eternal love, rather than the mortal beauty that disintegrates into dust. Herbert's response to Sidney coalesces in "Love" (II): "Our eies shall see thee, which before saw dust;/ ... All knees shall bow to thee; all wits shall rise,/ And praise him who did make and mend our eies." As Sidney proposed in the *Apology*, wits and eyes are dedicated to praising "Immortal Love, author of this great frame" ("Love" I, 1), not to the "love which reachest but to dust" ("Leave me," 1). Herbert alludes to Sidney's use of the words "fading" and "dust": "Sprung from that beautie which can never fade;/ How hath man parcel'd out thy glorious name,/ And thrown it on that dust which thou hast made" ("Love" I, lines 2–4).

   These passages from Sidney's works were in Herbert's mind when he announced the shape of his poetic career at the age of sixteen, as recorded in his sonnets to his mother:

> My God, where is that ancient heat towards thee,
> Wherewith whole showls of *Martyrs* once did burn,
> Besides their other flames? Doth Poetry
> Wear *Venus* Livery? only serve her turn?
> Why are not *Sonnets* made of thee? and layes   5
> Upon thine Altar burnt? Cannot thy love
> Heighten a spirit to sound out thy praise
> As well as any she? Cannot thy *Dove*
> Out-strip their *Cupid* easily in flight?
> Or, since thy wayes are deep, and still the same,   10

Will not a verse run smooth that bears thy name?
Why doth that fire, which by thy power and might
    Each breast doth feel, no braver fuel choose
    Than that, which one day Worms may chance refuse?

Sure, Lord, there is enough in thee to dry
  Oceans of *Ink*; for, as the Deluge did
  Cover the Earth, so doth thy Majesty:
Each Cloud distills thy praise, and doth forbid
Poets to turn it to another use.   5
Roses and *Lillies* speak thee; and to make
A pair of Cheeks of them, is thy abuse.
Why should I *Womens eyes* for Chrystal take?
Such poor invention burns in their low mind
Whose fire is wild, and doth not upward go   10
To praise, and on thee, Lord, some *Ink* bestow.
Open the bones, and you shall nothing find
    In the best *face* but *filth*, when, Lord, in thee
    The *beauty* lies in the *discovery*.

The first sonnet commemorates the martyrs throughout Christian history and also perhaps the more recent Protestant heretics burned in England under Catholic rule: "My God, where is that ancient heat towards thee, / Wherewith whole showls of *Martyrs* once did burn,/ Besides their other flames?"[10] The poem yearns for the heat felt by a martyr, primarily the passion to announce one's faith in obedient sacrifice, as well as the "other", secondary flames of the destructive fire. If the poem refers to English history, then it castigates the descent of verse into trivial eroticism as a sign of the prostitution of the Protestant cause: "Doth Poetry/ Wear *Venus* Livery? only serve her turn?" Both poems become heated in their rejection of female beauty as a legitimate subject for poetry: "Why should I *Womens eyes* for Chrystal take?/ Such poor invention burns in their low mind/ Whose fire is wild, and doth not upward go/ To praise, and on thee, Lord, some *Ink* bestow." This last passage shows knowledge of Gascoigne's "Certayne notes of Instruction", with its account of invention: "If I should undertake to wryte in prayse of a gentlewoman, I would neither praise hir christal eye, or hir cherrie lippe, etc. For these things are *trita & obvia*."[11] "Invention" in the study of rhetoric referred not to a nineteenth-century sense of artistic creativity, but to the "finding out" of ways to express one's topic, for instance, the beauty of a woman. The young Herbert claims that celebrations of the "Chrystal" eye of a woman have become lifeless because they are divorced from the true source of inspiration: "*Roses* and *Lillies* speak thee; and to make/ A pair of Cheeks of them, is thy abuse".

Herbert's early sonnets announce the religious trajectory of his interests as a lyric poet, but they also include harsh attacks on the female body as deceptively beautiful but actually repulsive. Sonnet I laments the precedence of physical passion over spiritual: "Cannot thy love/ Heighten a spirit to sound out thy praise/ As well as any she? ... Why doth that fire, which by thy power and might/ Each breast does feel, no braver fuel choose/ Than that, which one day Worms may chance refuse?" (6–8, 12–14). Sonnet II is more graphic: "Open the bones, and you shall nothing find/ In the best *face* but *filth*, when, Lord, in thee/ The *beauty* lies in the *discovery*" (12–14). Herbert addresses the blazon of female beauty that is conventional to the sonnet in which each part of a woman's face is compared to a beautiful object of nature, but he ends with a violent unmasking reminiscent of Spenser in which the beautiful Duessa turns into a filthy hag.[12] We might conjecture that this aggressive rejection of women, edited out of the later "Love" I and II, was linked to Herbert's reaction against his mother's marriage to John Danvers in 1609, especially because Magdalene Herbert was forty and Danvers twenty, only four years older than George. Perhaps these promises to his mother to write only about sacred love were a means of sublimating sexual energy to the task of scholarly achievement, since Herbert had entered Cambridge some months before. But such explanations leave out the entirely customary aggression against women inherent to the denunciation of physical love, as a poem by Edward Herbert makes clear:

> Be the nut brown,
> The loveliest colour which the flesh doth crown,
> I'll think it like a Nut – a fair outside,
> Within which worms and rottenness abide ...
> If any yet will think their beauties best ...
> ... [Death,] send chosen bands
> Of Worms, your soldiers, to their fairest hands,

And make them leprous, scabb'd: upon their face
Let those your Pioneers, Ringworms, take their place ...
("To his Mistress [Death] for her true Picture")[13]

So Hamlet meditates on Yorick's skull, "Now get you to my lady's chamber and tell her, let her paint an inch thick, to this favour she must come."[14] In his "answers" to William Herbert, Benjamin Rudyerd describes love, "The greatest and most conceal'd Imposter/ That ever vain Credulity did foster."[15] Arguments against love were conventionally gendered: love fools men into worshipping female beauty; women obsessed with the power of their beauty are reminded of the skull beneath the skin. Poets are male; the bodies seen or bringing "fading pleasure" are female. In Sidney's *Arcadia*, Musidorus debates with Pyrocles over the value of love, and Musidorus associates the "vile infection" of love with the weakness of women.[16] The poetic debate between Rudyerd and William Herbert in their collection takes its cue from this passage in the *Arcadia*. For Rudyerd, "This baseness is to man, the greatest curse ... How can we so unman our selves, and fall/ Beneath that creature which was made of all/ Next under us ..."[17] Although the cross-dressed Pyrocles defends love by defending women in the *Arcadia*, Sidney's "Leave me, O love" renounces "splendid trifles": "Whatever fades, but fading pleasure brings."[18] By 1610 the members of the Sidney-Herbert coterie had rather fully mapped out the way for a young man interested in the repudiation of the secular love lyric.

The "Jordan" poems in *The Temple* provide further evidence that Herbert's decision to shape his literary career as a poet of sacred love was formulated in response to issues associated with his relatives' literary circle. The word "Jordan" in Herbert's work offers the Biblical river as an alternative to the Greek "Helicon". For early modern poets, "Helicon" referred to fountains of water sacred to the classical Muses and capable of providing poetic inspiration. *England's Helicon* was an anthology of pastoral verse published in 1600 and reprinted in 1614, and filled with poems by Sidney and others imitating him. The volume announced in Latin on the title page, "Come with pure garment and pure hands, and take the water of the fountain."[19] Herbert counters with a Biblical kind of purity and inspiration: the Jordan river was associated with Naaman's healing of leprosy

(2 Kings 5:10) and John's baptism of Jesus (Matt. 3:13–17). Thomas
Lodge writes in 1596,

> Now at last after I have wounded the world with too much surfeit
> of vanity I may be by the true Helicon, cleansed from the leprosy
> of my lewd lines, and being washed in the Jordan of Grace,
> employ my labours to the comfort of the faithful.[20]

Unlike Sidney, Herbert's language was to be cleansed from the
outset from the taint of erotic love and elaborate artifice, and
sanctified for the inspired expression of religious truth.

But the Jordan poems are not merely a rebuke to Sidney as a love
poet, since they also include complimentary imitations of his poetry
and strong signs of Herbert's interest in the group of poets
surrounding Sidney's cultural heir, the earl of Pembroke. "Jordan"
(I) begins as a wit contest in which the speaker "answers" imaginary
poets advocating contemporary styles, particularly the "fiction" of
the pastoral, associated with Sidney through the *Arcadia* and
England's Helicon. But Herbert's poem also uses the "plain" style
developed by Sidney in his sonnets (#15) as well as by Shakespeare
(#21). Whereas Herbert uses this style for religious purposes, his
plainness, like that of his predecessors, is in no way simple:

> Who sayes that fictions onely and false hair
> Become a verse? Is there in truth no beautie?
> Is all good structure in a winding stair?
> May no lines passe, except they do their dutie
>   Not to a true, but painted chair?
>
> Is it no verse, except enchanted groves
> And sudden arbours shadow course-spunne lines?
> Must purling streams refresh a lovers loves?
> Must all be vail'd, while he that reades, divines,
>   Catching the sense at two removes?
>
> Shepherds are honest people; let them sing:
> Riddle who list, for me, and pull for Prime:
> I envie no mans nightingale or spring;
> Nor let them punish me with losse of rime,
>   Who plainly say, *My God, My King.*

Herbert follows Sidney by rejecting the habits of conventional poets, "You that do search for every purling spring" *(Astrophil and Stella*, #15). Just as Sidney uses phrases that illustrate these failures ("running in rattling rows", 15.6), so Herbert parodies bad pastoral verse ("Must purling streams refresh a lovers loves?", 8). Like Sidney, Herbert imagines a plain style that is inspired and impassioned ("You ... do bewray a want of inward touch", 15.9–10), as well as figurative. "Fictions" or metaphors are acceptable; "false hair" (1) and "winding stair" (3) are perfect examples. These figures are taken from the excesses of the courtier and the country house, and represent the hollowness of verbal complexity for its own sake. But while metaphors are acceptable, "fictions onely" are not. Both Herbert and Sidney celebrate true feeling rather than poetic artifice, but Herbert departs from Sidney by including pastoral love as one of these fictions. The entire apparatus of the pastoral world, with its shepherds, love songs, and indirect political commentary, is rejected in favor of a poetry which may be condensed, enigmatic, and figurative, but which nevertheless is explicit in its religious commitment. Speakers of this "truth" have no patience for the indirectness of pastoral allegory ("Must all be vail'd, while he that reades, divines,/ Catching the sense at two removes?", 9–10). Nor do they pay reverence to a false aesthetic standard ("May no lines passe, except they do their dutie/ Not to a true, but painted chair?", 4–5). Herbert creates an allegory in small, in which "lines", like courtiers, bow before or or yield obedience to an officer or authority. "Painted chair" recalls Plato's critique of poets whose images create a level twice removed from real "ideas", but the phrase also suggests Shakespeare's "painted beauty" of sonnet #21, perhaps a woman with make-up, but more generally the entire Petrarchan aesthetic itself. Herbert thus refuses to bow before the fashion of pastoral and Petrarchan verse, and joins Shakespeare in advocating being a poet "true in love" who will "truly write" (21.9). But, for Herbert, that truth and its beauty spring from loyalties that are sacred and, to him, metaphysically sound: *"My God, My King"* (15).

The poem is finally not plain at all, but quite elusive. Does the last line mean "my God and my King", in which case it becomes an announcement of allegiance to the monarch without pastoral indirectness? Or does it mean "my God is my King", and courtly convention an empty fiction? Certainly each stanza is just as riddling as any pastoral allegory. The ending is not preachy, but even a bit cavalier, staging a truce between rival poetic factions. The poem's serious search for a trustworthy relationship between metaphysical "truth" and beautiful language includes a calculated use of quips.

Herbert constructs an autobiographical story in "Jordan" (II) that turns the wit of the Sidney-Herbert circle into clever but earnest self-reflection. Significantly revised and linked with "Jordan" (I) through a change in the title, the poem reconsiders the problems of an overly artificial poetic aesthetic explored by Sidney (*Astrophil and Stella*, #1, 3, 15), Shakespeare (#21), and Herbert in "Jordan" (I). It finds that questionable artifice is not simply the province of the secular love poet writing in the pastoral or Petrarchan mode, but also the pitfall of a religious poet:

> When first my lines of heav'nly joyes made mention,
> Such was their lustre, they did so excell,
> That I sought out quaint words, and trim invention;
> My thoughts began to burnish, sprout, and swell,
> Curling with metaphors a plain intention,
> Decking the sense, as if it were to sell.
>
> Thousands of notions in my brain did runne,
> Off'ing their service, if I were not sped,
> I often blotted what I had begunne;
> This was not quick enough, and that was dead,
> Nothing could seem too rich to clothe the sunne,
> Much lesse those joyes which trample on his head.
>
> As flames do work and winde, when they ascend,
> So did I weave myself into the sense.
> But while I bustled, I might heare a friend
> Whisper, *How wide is all this long pretense!*
> *There is in love a sweetnesse readie penn'd:*
> *Copie out onely that, and save expense.*

Just as the speaker in "Jordan" (I) wants to "plainly say, *My God, My King*", so "Jordan" (II) disapproves of "Curling with metaphors a plain intention" (5). But the offending metaphors in "Jordan" (II) are not those of tired Petrarchan convention used to praise secular love, but rather the productions of the speaker-poet's overly fertile imagination used to describe sacred love. Sidney (#15) and Herbert in the first Jordan poem give examples of the clichés of the poetic styles they criticize; "Jordan" (II) provides a model of original and stunningly awkward artifice: "Nothing could seem too rich to clothe the sun,/ Much less those joyes which trample on his head" (11–12). Such swelling thoughts (4) explain why the second line of the poem includes a confusion about the reference of the word "lustre": one wonders what the speaker finds most excellent, "heavenly joyes" or his lines about them (1)? This ambiguity illuminates the poet's self-absorption before the "friend" interrupts him.

As with all poems proclaiming the value of the plain style, it is difficult to assess what the new, baptized style will be like. But, as with Sidney and "Jordan" (I), it is clear that this style will remain figurative. The ending of "Jordan" (II) alludes to *Astrophil and Stella*, #1 and 3. Sidney's poems seek authentic, vivid language, and reject conventional artifice for words directly inspired by beauty. Sidney's famous first sonnet ends with an energetic, startling interruption, "'Fool,' said my muse to me; 'look in thy heart, and write'" (1.14). The third poem offers a solution through the figure of "copying", "in Stella's face I read/ What love and beauty be; then all my deed/ But copying is, what in her nature writes" (3.12–14). To "copy" what one reads in a face (Sidney) or to "copy" the sweetness ready penned in divine love (Herbert, 16–18): these are witty and complex figurative expressions. Although Herbert implies that metaphor has the power to distract by calling attention to itself (5), neither he nor Sidney renounces metaphor but rather each uses the image of copying to assert an exact transference from one mode to another, either from a beautiful face to beautiful words, or from the power of love to a powerful expression of it. These "plain" styles therefore use figures that claim to be precise in their subordination to the subject, but nevertheless compelling in their evocation of it.

"Jordan" (II) is an "answer-poem" that responds to Sidney with reproof (by replacing Petrarchan love with divine love) and compliment (by adopting his strategies for the plain style). But it is likely that the poem alludes as well to Shakespeare's sonnets, and, indirectly, to William Herbert's coterie. The sixth line of "Jordan" (II), "Decking the sense as if it were to sell," seems to refer rather directly to the last line of Shakespeare's sonnet #21: "I will not praise that purpose not to sell," especially since Herbert originally wrote "Praising" rather than "Decking". Both poets associate ornate verse with vulgar profit seeking. Although Shakespeare's line has been described as "proverbial",[21] the likelihood of an allusion to Shakespeare by Herbert is made stronger by the fact that both poems refer to Sidney's sonnets (particularly #3 and 15). Herbert's allusions to Sidney and Shakespeare could be approached as an example of a purely aesthetic "anxiety of influence", but that all three poets were linked to the Sidney-Herbert circle. This suggests that a more social, coterie form of answering is taking place in "Jordan" (II).

Shakespeare certainly received patronage from William Herbert, and there is strong evidence that Shakespeare's sonnets were important to the Sidney-Herbert circle. The dedication of the First Folio of Shakespeare's plays to "the incomparable paire of brethren" William and Philip Herbert notes that they "prosequuted both [the plays] and their Author living, with so much favour."[22] The theory that William Herbert was the "Mr. W.H." to whom the Shakespeare's sonnets were dedicated has a long history, and has been endorsed by Katherine Duncan-Jones, who provides plentiful circumstantial evidence in support of it. She notes that William Herbert alludes to Shakespeare's sonnet #116 in the opening verse in the Herbert-Rudyerd poetic debate discussed above. She also claims that George Herbert's sonnets to his mother may include a shocked response to the homoeroticism and cynical heterosexuality of Shakespeare's recently published sonnets, as well as specific references to them.[23] But if this is so, then the Jordan poems offer as well an elegant compliment to Shakespeare's development of a plain style that provides a model for Herbert in its imitation of and contesting with that of Sidney.

Like Herbert, Shakespeare follows Sidney by using examples of the kind of poetic style he condemns, but Shakespeare's example criticizes Sidney as well, "my love is as fair/ As any mother's child, though not so bright/ As those gold candles fixed in heaven's air" (21.10–12). "Gold candles" is a metaphor characteristic of those satirized by the poem "who heaven itself for ornament doth use" (21.3), but it also refers to Stella, or star, Sidney's name for the beloved. Shakespeare shows that Sidney was not so "plain" as he claimed to be (*Astrophil and Stella*, #15). Herbert's poet-speaker has "heav'nly joyes" (1) to justify using heaven as ornament, but he finds that a religious subject is no guarantee against the verbal opulence that aims at selling itself and its writer rather than focusing on its topic. Despite Herbert's condemnation of "usurping lust" ("Love" II, 12), "Jordan" (II) represents "sacred parody" as potentially driven by an equally troublesome desire, here a lust for recognition. The last line of "Jordan" (II) may refer to Shakespeare's sonnet #129: "Th'expense of spirit in a waste of shame/ Is lust in action." In "Jordan" (II) the "friend" offers relief from the wasteful efforts of ambition, "Copie out onely that, and save expense." The poem acknowledges the lack of self-awareness in the poet's earlier denunciations of secular love, as it also courteously maps out a lineage for itself, including Sidney, Shakespeare, and William Herbert's coterie.

One poem can reveal the coterie nature of verse during this period. Earlier critics found it difficult to accept the poem as George Herbert's, but recent scholarship has provided evidence of its authenticity.[24] If this is Herbert's poem, then it is the only one we have by him on secular love. Attributed to him in one manuscript and one printed book associated with Cambridge is "Aethiopissa ambit Cestum Diversi Coloris Virum" ["A negro maid woos Cestus, a man of a different color."] The poem appears after an English poem addressed to Lord Chancellor Francis Bacon. This dates the poem to 1618-21. The English poem describes an exchange of gifts – a diamond from Bacon and "a Blackamore" from the writer, most probably the Latin poem. In the Latin poem, the black woman constructs arguments in defense of blackness. F.E. Hutchinson seems torn about the poem's attribution to Herbert; he places the Latin poem with Herbert's other Latin verse, but the English poem is in the section on "Doubtful Poems". Nevertheless Hutchinson makes it clear that, whoever the writer is, the Latin poem appeared in later manuscripts with imitations or "answers" to it, including "The Boyes Answer to the Blackmoor", and "A Faire Nymph scorning a Black Boy courting her". The poems in praise of blackness by Shakespeare and Edward Herbert suggest as well that the topic was fashionable among poetic wits.[25]

The praise of blackness was a version of the paradox topos through which young English writers sought to publicize their verbal powers. John Donne is best known for his paradoxes ("The Autumnal", supposedly on Magdalene Herbert, is a paradox poem), but they are to be found in almost all seventeenth-century miscellanies. The Herbert-Rudyerd volume includes "A Paradox in praise of a painted Woman".[26] Often praising what common wisdom condemns, the form displays the inventiveness and rhetorical skill required of students in the schools and universities, like Westminster and Cambridge. The paradox is associated with the disputed question, since students exercised their wits at developing arguments on both sides of the issue.[27] None of the poems on blackness should be considered serious protestations against bigotry; they instead announce the ability of the poet to fabricate a reasonable argument on what was considered a questionable topic.

The poem attributed to George Herbert develops the positive attributes of blackness despite the conventional exaltation of fairness as the model for female beauty. He may have been influenced by his brother Edward's numerous poems on the subject, "Nor are thy hair and eyes made of that ruddy beam/ Or golden-sanded stream/ Which we find still the vulgar Poet's theme,/ But reverend black ..."[28] Perhaps George's poem isn't so radically different from the sonnets to his mother, since all three question the Petrarchan standard of praise to a golden haired, fair-complected woman. But the Latin poem is primarily interested in listing arguments in favor of blackness:

> ... hoc, Ceste, colore
> Sunt etiam tenebrae, quas tamen optat amor ...
> Si nigro sit terra solo, quis despicit aruum?
> Cum mihi sit facies fumus, quas pectore flammas ...
> Iamdudum tacitè delituisse putes?
> Dure, negas? O fata mihi praesaga doloris,
> Quae mihi lugubres contribuere genas! (1–2,5,9–12)

[Dark, O Cestus, has this color too, but love/ wants it anyway ... Who despises/ The furrow if the land is black? ... Because my face is smoke,/ What fires do you think have hid within my heart/ So long in silence now? O stony man,/ Do you say no? O Fates who gave me/ Mournful cheeks, fortelling my affliction!][29]

The poem attributed to Herbert includes echoes of Shakespeare. The "lugubres ... genas" (12) or "mournful cheeks" recall the "two mourning eyes" of the dark lady (#132; also 127). But even more tellingly, Shakespeare's sonnet #131 begins by overturning the standard of beauty, but ends with a reassertion of the traditional association between blackness and evil: "In nothing art thou black save in thy deeds,/ And thence this slander, as I think, proceeds" (12–14). So "Aethiopissa" begins by questioning cultural views, but returns to blackness as curse.

This poem is uncharacteristic of Herbert not only in its subject matter, but in its role-playing. But it is useful to be reminded of the rituals of exchange and imitation surrounding upper-class poetry as well as university collections in the seventeenth century. Perhaps it is not so difficult to imagine Herbert exchanging gifts with Bacon, acting as an academic wit, and trying out his hand at a paradox poem on blackness, especially given its current popularity.[30]

This context can also illuminate the debt of Herbert's religious poems to coterie topics, and clarify that his analysis of spiritual states developed not in private but in relationship to a group of writers and an audience. "A Parodie" proves conclusively that George Herbert responded to the network of coterie exchange. Although some doubt remains about the authorship of "Soules Joy", it is clear that "A Parodie" answers this poem, which is linked in subject matter and language to many other verses of the time. These include Donne's "Valediction: forbidding Mourning"; "Absence", widely attributed to John Hoskyns; the numerous other examples of "absence" poems in miscellanies like *A Poetical Rhapsody*; and Sidney's "Oft have I mused" and the poems on absence #88, 89, 105 and 106 in *Astrophil and Stella*. Most commentators have concluded that "Soules Joy" is by William Herbert. Summers writes "Although the editing of Pembroke's poems in 1660 was notoriously careless, the younger John Donne would hardly have attributed to William Herbert a poem written by his father." "A Parodie", then, is an instance of sacred parody explicitly used to evoke the context of coterie poetry, and probably the Sidney-Herbert coterie. George Herbert answers a poem thoroughly imbedded in the networks of poetic exchange and associated with the coterie topic of "mutual love".[31]

The most famous poem on this topic is Donne's "Valediction: forbidding Mourning", which offers the woman addressed a spiritual bond as an antidote to separation:

> Dull sublunary lovers love
>> (Whose soule is sense) cannot admit
> Absence, because it doth remove
>> Those things which elemented it.
>
> But we by'a love, so much refin'd
>> That our selves know not what it is,
> Inter-assured of the mind,
>> Care lesse, eye, lips, and hands to misse.[32] (13–24)

Donne celebrates a bond made of souls not bodies, since the lovers are linked through a mutual confidence that does not require contact through the physical senses ("eye, lips, and hands"). This makes the love strong enough to endure separation. It is unlikely that Donne's topic is original, since many wrote similar poems:

> Absence hear my protestation
>> Against thy strengthe
>> Distance and lengthe,
> Doe what thou canst for alteration;
>> For harts of truest mettall
>> Absence doth joyne, and time doth settle.[33] (1–6)

Edward Herbert contributed his own poem on the topic in 1608:

> But since I must depart, and that our love
>> Springing at first but in an earthly mould,
> Transplanted to our souls, now doth remove
>> Earthly effects, what time and distance would,
>> Nothing now can our loves allay ...[34]

It is most likely William Herbert who responded with "Soules Joy":

> Soules joy, now I am gone,
>> And you alone,

> (Which cannot be,
> Since I must leave my selfe with thee,
> And carry thee with me)
> Yet when unto our eyes
> Absence denyes
> Each others sight,
> And makes to us a constant night,
> When others change to light;
> *O give no way to griefe,*
> *But let beliefe*
> *Of mutual love,*
> *This wonder to the vulgar prove*
> *Our Bodyes, not wee move.* (1–15)[35]

All four poems consider "absence" as an enemy to affection, and counter with a *"mutual love"* far superior to that cast in "an earthly mould" and felt by "dull sublunary lovers." This spiritualized love stems from a union of hearts or souls: *"Our Bodyes, not wee move."*

George Herbert uses these poems to formulate in "A Parodie" an account of the spiritual intimacy between God and man. Rosemond Tuve has convincingly argued that the poems by William and George were written as songs to be sung, perhaps as evening entertainments.[36] But George turns the occasion as well into an opportunity for introspection:

> Souls joy, when thou art gone,
> And I alone,
> Which cannot be,
> Because thou dost abide with me,
> And I depend on thee;
>
> Yet when thou dost suppresse
> The cheerfulnesse
> Of thy abode,
> And in my powers not stirre abroad,
> But leave me to my load;
>
> O what a damp and shade
> Doth me invade!
> No stormie night

Can so afflict or so affright,
        As thy eclipsed light.

Ah Lord! do not withdraw,
        Lest want of aw
        Make Sinne appeare;
And when thou dost but shine lesse cleare,
        Say, that thou art not here.

And then what life I have,
        While Sinne doth rave,
        And falsly boast,
That I may seek, but thou art lost;
        Thou and alone thou know'st.

O what a deadly cold
        Doth me infold!
        I half beleeve,
That Sinne sayes true: but while I grieve,
        Thou com'st and dost relieve.

When juxtaposed with lyrics on mutual love, George Herbert's poem is remarkable in taking on the position of the person left behind, traditionally the woman,[37] and in transposing mutual love into the dilemmas of spirituality. From William Herbert's poem, George adopts the imagery of light and dark in evoking a contrast between joy and cheerfulness as opposed to grief and doubt. Although Herbert's religious verse may have the stronger metaphysical basis for claiming that the two parties never actually separate, his poem includes the most disturbing portraits of emotional distress. As Tuve has pointed out, "A Parodie" is organized around the similar stanzas three and six, both of which evoke the speaker's suffering. Tuve suggests that both are refrains for the preceding two stanzas of the song,[38] but they also move far beyond the confident assurances of the secular poems: "O what a damp and shade/ Doth me invade! ... O what a deadly cold/ Doth me infold!" The third stanza develops an image important to several other Herbert poems, including "The Flower" and "Affliction" (I): "No stormie night/ Can so afflict or so affright,/ As thy eclipsed light." The grief of a woman anxious that her lover won't return because of death or inconstancy turns into the frightened uncertainty of a religious man who begins to doubt his salvation or the existence of God: "Ah Lord! do not withdraw/ Lest want of aw/ Make Sinne appeare;/ And when thou dost but shine lesse clear,/ Say that thou art not here." Herbert has used the "absence" motif to map out a complex spiritual state. This will not be news to Herbert critics. But it is worth considering that this "sacred parody" was probably imagined as an answering song, that is, conceived not in private meditation, but for the purposes of performance before an audience. Furthermore, it may have been received by William Herbert as a witty entry into his family coterie's continual juxtaposition of secular and sacred love. It definitely displays George Herbert's knowledge of coterie ritual. This suggests that, despite our modern prejudices, seventeenth-century coterie performance and religious introspection could occur simultaneously.[39]

Other Herbert poems are linked to the Sidney-Herbert coterie. The second part of "Christmas" reinvents a Sidney poem in *The Arcadia*. George Herbert's "Clasping of Hands" and William Herbert's "Had I loved butt att that rate" play on the rhyming words "mine" and "thine".[40] Herbert's autobiographical "Affliction" (I) depends on *Astrophil and Stella*, #61. "The Answer" responds to *A&S*, #21. Whereas Maureen Quilligan has demonstrated that several of Mary Wroth's poems respond to John Donne, R.E. Pritchard suggests that Herbert's "Flower" may be indebted to Wroth's "Forbear dark night" and "The spring now come at last".[41]

2
Cambridge and University Works

In 1610, during his first year at Cambridge, Herbert announced his design to write religious verse characteristic of the Sidney-Herbert circle. In his University writings of 1612–1623, he signaled his dedication to international Protestantism, as well as his interest in high office in church or state. His views about church issues were those of the Elizabethan settlement and King James – Calvinist in theology and conformist in church structure and ceremony. At times he aligned himself with positions and people closer to Anglo-Catholicism. For instance, he opposed war with Catholic Spain and dedicated one work to the Arminian Lancelot Andrewes. However I will argue that these were the exceptions to the rule, and may have been the result not of personal conviction but politic strategy. On the whole and in the vast majority of cases, Herbert expressed his commitment to a Protestant England and its potential as an imperial power.

This period of Herbert's life has traditionally been approached as his "worldly" period before the more "meditative" withdrawal into Wiltshire. The works he wrote during this time have primarily been considered for evidence of ambition, interest in patronage, and willingness to flatter those in high office. But these works display a consistent interest in the success of international Protestantism, an interest Herbert maintained until the end of his life.[1] Analysis of these works will reveal a surprising use of imagery from Virgil's *Aeneid*, and an identification of England with the victorious imperial powers of ancient Greece and Rome.

During this period, Protestants pursued their goal of establishing the religion worldwide. They fought to defeat "Papism" in the

Thirty Years' War, and competed with Spain over colonization of the Americas. Philip Sidney represented to English Protestants the brilliant courtier-warrior dying in action, and his nephew William Herbert inherited Sidney's position as a leading spokesperson for the cause in the royal court and through patronage of Protestant writers and clerics. William influenced Parliament through his representatives in the Commons, including Benjamin Rudyerd, Edward Herbert, John Danvers, and George Herbert. William invested in the Virginia Company to spread the word and to increase his wealth, and others in his circle did the same, including his brother Philip, John Danvers (George's step-father), and John Donne.

When George Herbert entered Trinity College, Cambridge, on May 1609, soon after his sixteenth year, he moved from the high-church Westminster School, which included as deans the Arminians Lancelot Andrewes and Richard Neile, to a far more Calvinist Trinity.[2] His master at Westminster School predicted Herbert's success: he entered as a Westminster Scholar with a quarterly pension, receiving his Bachelor of Arts in 1613 and Master of Arts in 1616. He was appointed sublector in rhetoric in 1617 and Praelector in rhetoric in 1618. After serving as deputy Orator for Cambridge in 1619, he was elected to the position of Public Orator in 1620.[3]

I. "Activ'st spirit": Poems on the death of Henry, Prince of Wales, 1612

On November 6, 1612, the eldest son of King James died of typhoid fever. George Herbert wrote two Latin poems on the occasion, the first of his poems to be printed. That these poems were included in a Cambridge volume honoring Prince Henry suggests that Herbert, even at the age of nineteen, was highly valued as a Latinist by the University.[4] The poems he wrote a few months before he received his Bachelor of Arts degree reveal his proficiency as a poet of nationalism. The death of Prince Henry created a crisis of confidence for English Protestants, and, in his poems, Herbert reassures his readers that the state's religious mission is divinely ordained.

Henry Stuart was created Prince of Wales in June 1610 and given his own household and palaces. He had already risen into prominence as a symbol of the Protestant cause. Although James I was committed to peace with Spain, Henry made no secret of his militant dedication to Continental Protestantism, as well as his sister's marriage to the German Protestant prince, Frederick, Elector Palatine. Many saw him as the savior sent by God to defend His church. According to Beaulieu in Paris, "... God had reserved and destined him *as a chosen Instrument to be the Standard-bearer of his Quarrel in these miserable times, to work the Restoration of his Church and the Destruction of the Romish idolatry"*. Sir John Holles spoke of Henry's Protestant activism: "For our home preservation he held up religion and held in the presumptuous papist ... the industrious spirit was comforted: all actions profitable or honorable for the kingdom were fomented by him, witness the North West passage, Virginia, Guiana, the Newfoundland, etc., to all which he gave his money as well as his good word." John Donne's elegy on Henry coordinated the militancy of the Prince with the peacemaking of his father: he "was his great fathers greatest instrument,/ and activ'st spirit, to convey and tie/ This soule of peace, through Christianity" (32–34).[5] Any potential conflict between the foreign policy of father and son is resolved in this formulation, since the son's industrious actions, including war, are imagined as resulting in the father's goal of peace.

Herbert's Latin poems, entitled "In Obitum Henrici Principis Walliae" ["On the death of Henry, Prince of Wales"] reinforce Protestant imperial hopes by linking England to Greece and Rome, and Prince Henry to the classical epic hero. Dismissing the Muses as powerless, the speaker in the first poem calls on his own mind and spirit to ask why God has allowed such a hero to die, in a question reminiscent of Virgil's *Aeneid*:

Quare age, Mens, effare, precor, quo numine laeso?
Quae suberant causae? quid nos committere tantum,
Quod non Lanigerae pecudes, non Agmina lustrent?
Annon longa fames miseraéque iniuria pestis
Poena minor fuerat, quàm fatum Principis aegrum? (17–21)

[And so awaken,
Intellect, divulge, I ask you, what it was
That gave offense to God, what the underlying reasons were,
What sin on our part was so great
No beast of wool, no stream could cleanse it?

Would not have famine or the plague's bleak
Visitation been a lesser punishment
Than the Prince's painful fate?][6]

Herbert echoes the beginning of the *Aeneid*:

> Musae mihi causas memora quo numine laeso
> quidve dolens regina deum tot volvere casus
> insignem pietate virum tot adire labores
> impulerit. tantaene animis caelestibus irae?

[Tell me, O Muse, the cause; wherein thwarted in will or wherefore angered, did the Queen of heaven drive a man, of goodness so wondrous, to traverse so many perils, to face so many toils. Can heavenly spirits cherish resentment so dire?][7]

Herbert repeats Virgil's phrase "quo numine laeso" ("as a result of what injury to divinity") to seek a cause for apparent divine injustice, and to identify the death of Prince Henry with the sufferings of Aeneas.[8] This allusion also suggests that, despite this cruel event, the imperial power of Rome could be part of England's future as it was for Aeneas' descendants. Certainly the country had placed all its grand hopes on the prince, "... nostra infortunia tantùm/ Fatáque Fortunásque & spem laesêre futuram" (24–25). ["Our misfortunes only/ Have wounded fate and luck and future hope."] The speaker wonders why Henry died so young even though he had been spared in the Gunpowder plot in 1605, when Catholics tried to destroy the royal family and Parliament, "Quare etiam nuper Pyrij de pulueris ictu/ Principis innocuam seruastis numina Vitam,/ Vt morbi perimant, alióque in puluere prostet?" (33–35). ["Why too of late, O God,/ Did you preserve the Prince's life unscathed/ From the shock of burning dust, in order that disease/ Might snuff it out, in order that he might/ Be demonstrated in another dust?"] Herbert expresses the dismay Protestants felt at Henry's death since the prince's deliverance during the Gunpowder plot seemed to be a sign of God's support for their cause. The grief in the poem could be explained by a simple anxiety about succession (26–27), yet if so it suggests that only Prince Henry and not King James's remaining son Charles could provide security from Protestant enemies: "Quid non mutatum est?" (43) ["What has not changed?"].[9]

The second poem poses the same questions in a different way, and finds a tentative answer. Although the Muses had been rejected in the first poem as a source of inspiration, the speaker now addresses "Virgin Pallas", Minerva, the goddess of wisdom and defensive war, who inspires the Greek and Latin Muses: "dulcis ... Camoenae Pieridis Latiaéque Musae" (3–4). Although Herbert uses Pallas Athena and the Muses to represent the wisdom of Cambridge in other poems (to Frederick, Elector Palatine), here her patronage is for "you and yours", (5) and this includes the royal family. The poem draws a direct line of inheritance from Ancient Greece and Rome to England, as Athena becomes the patron saint of England as well as Athens. When the speaker asks Zeus's daughter why she can't protect her people from death, Athena answers: "Eia, ne metuas, precor,/ Nam fata non iustis repugnant/ Principibus, sed amica fiunt" (26–28). ["Ai, don't be/ Frightened, I beg you, for the Fates/ Are not against just princes, / But become their friends."][10] The poem leaves open the possibility that some kind of human crime has brought on the prince's death as a punishment, but it also reasserts the power of divine justice, assures readers that the national gods have not abandoned the English, and suggests that their epic task will be accomplished if their princes remain just.[11] Although the English have lost their hero, their mission remains the same: the defense of their country and the Protestant religion. The poem closes with an elegant image of how this lost branch of the royal family tree will be made into "the sweet/ Tibia" or flute, a source for epic song that will reveal Prince Henry's place in heaven and guide the country forward.

II. Herbert's poetic exchange with Donne: "In Sacram Anchoram Piscatoris"

At some point in their careers, John Donne and George Herbert exchanged Latin verses on Donne's seal of Christ crucified to an anchor. Most editors believe that the exchange took place soon after Donne was ordained on January 23, 1615. The new seal described in the poem also marked the letter Donne sent to Edward Herbert on the day of the ordination. Donne's poem to George illustrates either that a significant friendship already existed between the two, or that the poem itself offers such a bond. Donne's poem is notable because it predicts royal preferment for Herbert in the future.

Donne's poem rings inventive changes on the difference between cross and anchor, and the comparison between his old family crest of entwined serpents and the new seal he devised to mark his entrance into the priesthood. The new seal with Christ on an anchor represents the hope and stability conferred by grace: "Which hope we have as an anchor of the soul, both sure and stedfast, and which entereth into that within the veil; Whither the forerunner is for us entered, even Jesus, made an high priest for ever after the order of Melchisedec" (Heb. 6:19–20). Donne's new seal identifies him not with his human family but with the order of the priesthood, and as a priest he will both depend on Christ and imitate him by providing hope for his parishioners.

The poem says this in the most condensed and witty way:

> Hinc mihi Crux primo quae fronti impressa lavacro,
>   Finibus extensis, anchor a facta patet.
> Anchorae in effigiem Crux tandem desinit ipsam.
>   Anchora fir tandem Crux tolerata diu.
> Hoc tamen ut fiat, Christo vegetatur ab ipso
>   Crux, et ab Affixo, est Anchora facta, Iesu. (5–10)

> [The Crosse (my seal at Baptism) spred below,
> Does, by that form, into an Anchor grow.
> Crosses bear Anchors; Bear, as thou shouldst do
> Thy Crosse, and that Crosse grows an Anchor too.
> But he that makes our Crosses Anchors thus,
> Is Christ, who there is crucifi'd for us.][12]

The image of the cross spreading into an anchor is used as a teaching device: to suffer and learn through difficult experiences is to develop one's faith. But any implication that salvation can be earned is ruled out through a Calvinist emphasis on the one sacrifice of Christ. Donne acts the role of religious emblemist, autobiographer and minister. He teaches as well the virtues of wordplay and metaphysical wit. Herbert's mother and his brother Edward were well acquainted with Donne; the poet-minister may also have known of Herbert's interest in writing religious verse equal to the standards of the Sidney tradition. Donne's poem signals or perhaps offers a friendship between the two men based on their mutual acquaintances, their piety, and their verbal skill:

> Mitto nec exigua, exiguâ sub imagine, dona,
>   Pignora amicitiae, et munera; Vota, preces.
> Plura tibi accumulet, sanctus cognominis, Ille
>   Regia qui flavo Dona sigillat Equo. (19–22)

> [Under that little Seal great gifts I send,
>   {Wishes}, and prayers, pawns, and fruits of a friend,
> And may that Saint which rides in our great Seal,
>   To you, who bear his name, great bounties deal.]

The poem quips that the seal on the letter may be small, but the gifts sent in it are not, nor are these gifts material: pledges, offices, vows and prayers of friendship (20). The older Donne has given the younger Herbert advice, but also offered an alliance based on mutual interests, which include Protestant theology and an appreciation for complex religious verse. As one of the prayers of friendship, Donne predicts that royal gifts will be sent by the King (21–22), marked with the Great Seal of St. George, and provide George Herbert with the material abundance he needs and deserves.

Herbert answers in verse that is even more epigrammatic. His title is riddling in itself: "In Sacram Anchoram Piscatoris", or, on the sacred anchor of the fisherman. Herbert honors Donne for becoming a fisher of men through his ordination, as well as for the eloquence that had made him famous before and after that event:

> Quod Crux nequibat fixa, Clavíque additi,
> (Tenere Christum scilicet, ne ascenderet)
> Tuíue Christum deuocans facundia
> Vltra loquendi tempus; addit Anchora:
> Nec hoc abundè est tibi, nisi certae Anchorae

Addas sigillum: nempe Symbolum suae
Tibi debet Vnda & Terra certitudinis. (1–7)

[Although the Crosse could not Christ here detain,
Though nail'd unto't, but he ascends again,
Nor yet thy eloquence here keep him still,
But onely while thou speak'st; This Anchor will.
Nor canst thou be content, unlesse thou to
This certain Anchor adde a Seal, and so
The Water, and the Earth both unto thee
Doe owe the symbole of their certainty.[13]

Like Donne, Herbert plays on the contrast between cross and anchor. While Donne imagines crosses growing into anchors, in Herbert's poem, only the anchor rather than the cross can keep Christ on earth, since the anchor represents the transition from earth to heaven (Heb. 6:19–20). The poem praises Donne's eloquence as a preacher and a maker of emblems: not only the image of Christ on an anchor, but the seal itself become significant in Herbert's reading. Just as the anchor provides stability in the water, so a wax seal can make earthly things more secure.

Herbert's attitude toward Donne here is somewhat unclear. It includes admiration, but the gifts of friendship offered in Donne's poem are not explicitly accepted. Indeed, the poem seems more intent on imitating, or perhaps outdoing Donne in his wit and condensed style. Perhaps through this poetic imitation, Herbert signals that he and Donne are bound together through their attitudes toward religion and verse. Donne was certainly known for his obscurity. According to Drummond of Hawthornden, Ben Jonson confided, "Donne said to him, he wrote that epitaph on Prince Henry [in 1613] *Look to me Faith* to match Edward Herbert in obscureness".[14] Perhaps in his answer to Donne, George Herbert develops his own ability at this riddling style, characteristic of poems like "Jordan" (I).

According to Helen Gardner, the seven lines quoted above were written at the time Herbert received Donne's poem, after the ordination in 1615.[15] She believes that, later in life, Donne sent to Herbert one of the seals described in the poem, and that after Donne's death, Herbert wrote additional verses on the seal. These provide a significant contrast to the earlier poem in their emphasis on friendship:

> Munde, fluas fugiásque licet, nos nostráque fixi:
>   Deridet motus sancta catena tuos.
>   Quondam fessus Amor loquens Amato,
>   Tot & tanta loquens amica, scripsit :
>   Tandem & fessa manus, dedit sigillum.
>
> Suavis erat, qui scripta dolens lacerando recludi,
> Sanctius in Regno Magni credebat Amoris
> (In quo fas nihil est rumpi) donare sigillum. (8–15)
>
> [Let the world reel, we and all ours stand sure,
> This holy Cable's of all storms secure.
>   When Love being weary made an end
>   Of kinde Expressions to his friend,
>   He writ; when 's hand could write no more,
>   He gave the Seale, and so left o're.
> How sweet a friend was he, who being griev'd
> His letters were broke rudely up, believ'd
> 'Twas more secure in great Loves Common-weal
> (Where nothing should be broke) to adde a Seal.

Gardner comments that these lines are most likely separate Latin verses of one couplet and two triplets rather than a complete poem. The two triplets seem to be written after Donne's death in 1631. She notes as well the warm tone throughout these lines as opposed to the emphasis on conceit in the earlier poem.

Gardner's account is developed in order to oppose the view of Izaak Walton that Donne and Herbert wrote all these verses as Donne's death approached in 1631. Gardner seems correct to conclude rather that Donne wrote his poem soon after ordination in 1615, since he refers to obtaining new arms in the present tense ("nanciscor", 4). The anchor as an image itself alludes to "the order of Melchisedec" (Heb. 6:20), or the priesthood. Also it seems likely that his letter to Edward Herbert with the new seal dated on the day of ordination and the poem to George would be sent around the same time. Nevertheless we would do well to consider the possibility that Walton may be more accurate in his account. If so, then it would be fascinating to consider Donne praying for royal preferment for Herbert in 1631! This would support the view of those who see Herbert's early death as cutting short his career plans for high ecclesiastical office.

III. *Musae Responsoriae*

After Herbert had held several appointments at Cambridge, he wrote *Musae Responsoriae*, a set of epigrams defending the ceremonies of the Anglican Church against the criticism of a Scottish Presbyterian Andrew Melville. The work was an ambitious effort by the 27-year-old Herbert to become a spokesperson for King James and the established church. Although Herbert's defense of ceremony in 1620–21 clearly announced his position as a conformist to church tradition, Christopher Hodgkins has shown that the poems also confirmed Herbert's theological views as Calvinist, views shared by King James at least until mid-1622 and by Cambridge University until 1626.[16] In the poems, Puritanism is approached not as a theological issue, since all significant parties are Calvinist, but as disobedience to state and church authority.

Most critics have concluded for several reasons that *Musae Responsoriae* was written between 1620 and 1621: Melville's poems were reprinted in 1620; Herbert's poems are addressed to Melville, who died in 1621; and *Musae Responsoriae* is dedicated to the Bishop of Winchester, most logically Lancelot Andrewes, bishop in February 1619.[17] By 1620, Herbert had become Public Orator of Cambridge University, and a collection of Latin poems defending church liturgy would be appropriate, although not required from the Orator. The work is dedicated to King James, Prince Charles, and the Bishop of Winchester, but it seems to have been Herbert's idea, not the University's or that of a patron. Through the work Herbert attempts to secure the attention and patronage of king and prince.

Although Walton claimed that Herbert met and pleased King James at the courts held at Newmarket and Royston near Cambridge, there is no substantiating evidence for this claim.[18] Walton errs on the dates and events of the king's visits to Cambridge, and elaborates without evidence on the official letter and epigram that Herbert did write for King James in response to the gift of the king's Latin works to Cambridge on May 20, 1620.[19] There is in fact no evidence that Herbert received an office through patronage from the king before or after *Musae Responsoriae*, despite Donne's prediction. The poems do open with a dedication to James that refers to a time when "the light/ Of your grace and attention opened to me", but this could simply refer to the position of Public Orator itself, and the letters and presentations that the Orator would make to the king.[20] It is almost certain that the king was not a patron before Herbert became orator, since Herbert's English letters list a number of people called on for help in obtaining this position, including John Danvers, Francis Nethersole, Benjamin Rudyerd, and "my Lord", most probably William Herbert, earl of Pembroke (369–371). All of these people were associated with the Protestant cause at home and abroad, and many continued as patrons to Herbert throughout his life. Herbert's appeal to the king, prince and bishop should be seen as an attempt to extend his sources of patronage to the highest levels.

James Doelman has demonstrated that Herbert's poems addressed a very specific conflict that arose between the English and Scottish churches between 1618 and 1622.[21] Although both the English and the Scottish churches were Calvinist in theology, the Scottish church was Presbyterian, which included low-church liturgy and no bishops. At the Hampton Court Conference in 1604, and in opposition to the Millenary Petition, King James refused to bring Presbyterianism into the Anglican Church. The Scot Andrew Melville first wrote his epigrams in 1603–4 as a reaction to the hostile responses of Cambridge and Oxford Universities to the Millenary Petition. King James however sought full compliance from the Scots by reestablishing the episcopal system in Scotland in 1607, and, in August 1618, the Scottish General Assembly stacked with laymen passed the Perth Articles, which required Scottish observance of Anglican ritual. David Calderwood led the outcry by the Scots against the Articles, and in 1620 Calderwood reprinted Andrew Melville's epigrams against Anglican ceremony. Numerous works published between 1618 and 1622 defended the Perth articles, some attacked Melville, and some writers received significant rewards from the king. It was in this context that Herbert wrote *Musae Responsoriae*.

It could be argued that Herbert's dedication to Lancelot Andrewes, an explicit Arminian at the time, represents Herbert's Anglo-Catholicism. Herbert's official letter for Cambridge to Andrewes does display remarkable affection.[22] As an Arminian, Andrewes argued against the Calvinist doctrine of predestination and claimed that individuals could influence their salvation through their own merit. There were some very active English Arminians, including William Laud, and a few had announced their intentions to preach the new doctrine and match it with high-church ritual. However, in 1618, King James made it clear that he fully supported Calvinism through his sponsorship of the Synod of Dort, specifically arranged to oppose the threat of Dutch Arminian theology. Views expressed at Cambridge were particularly important to the king, who called some on the carpet for their Arminian views.[23] Despite his clear preference for Arminian theology, Lancelot Andrewes had not joined others in supporting the Dutch Arminians in 1618 and seemed content to defer to the king's opinion.[24] Historian Kenneth Fincham has drawn attention to James' policy of advocating Calvinism but supporting churchmen of a wide spectrum of views.[25] In dedicating his work to "His Excellency Our Father and Lord in Christ, the Bishop of Winchester", Herbert probably hoped for the aid of Andrewes, but he may also be acknowledging James's policy of tolerance. The poet may also be signaling his devotion to hierarchy both in the state and in the church rather than commenting in any way on theology.

In Herbert's dedications, particularly to King James, we confront a language of deference, flattery, and extravagant compliment no doubt appropriate to the occasion, but difficult for modern readers to appreciate:

> Watch how the sun on the mud
> Of the Nile ebbing away,
> Pushes up with its light a fresh
> Nation. Caesar, before the light
> Of your grace and attention opened to me,
> My Muse too was vile mud:
> But now, because of you, she is alive,
> She can creep along, and has the nerve
> To step up where you are the sun. (p. 3)

We might react against the inference that a poet speaking to a king is like an insect spontaneously generated by the sun, but this kind of extravagant compliment is characteristic of Herbert's writings as a Public Orator. Michael Schoenfeldt has illuminated the similarity between Herbert's deference before God and his deference toward the king. Here, the dedication to the king at the beginning of *Musae* uses the same language as the poem to God at the end:

> Once you, great God, bless
> With sweet dew him who writes,
> No futile labor makes it
> A painful time for him ...
> Even as the Nile, unaware
> Of dikes, overflows,
> Lovely in its flooding ...
> ... the pleasure that I give,
> If I give it, is all from you. (#40: 1–10, 14)

Herbert deliberately draws a connection between the blessings of a king and of God through his references to the Nile, and so flatters James I. In the poem to the king, the Nile becomes productive through the power of the sun. In the poem to God, the Nile represents God's power pouring forth. Nevertheless, both poems link poetic creativity with the fertility associated with the Nile, whether inspired by king or God. Herbert also makes visible a central topic in the poems: that church officials, like state officials, deserve respect because their position in the hierarchy reflects the authority of God. As King James in the dedication, so the office of bishop in #7 is compared to the sun, who "Surrounds the low earth/ With unfailing light".

Musae Responsoriae affirms the Calvinism shared by English and Scottish churches, but insists on obedience to the English model of church authority and ritual. As Hodgkins puts it, Herbert:

> ... begins his attack on the Scots Calvinist Andrew Melville by agreeing with Melville's theology and choice of 'sacred authors', including not only the ancient Fathers, but also Martyr, Bucer, Whitaker, and, of course, Calvin. All of them, as Herbert says of Melville and himself, 'revere the Divine Will' [#33, 4]. It is on

this common ground of predestinarian theology that Herbert engages the Puritans in controversy over church government and ritual.[26]

Herbert remarks in epigram #4 that he agrees with two-thirds of Melville's work. Only the first third warrants an aggressive answer, and that third challenges the authority of English king, bishop, and tradition:

> One part opposes sacred ritual;
> The second praises sacred authors;
> The third is full of God. About the latter two
> Our minds are in accord: I also praise
> Holy men; I, too, worship God.
> The first contentions only lend themselves
> To disagreement. (4:4–10)

In the epigrams, Herbert defends the "sacred rituals" of baptism, the sign of the cross, the loyalty oath to the Thirty-Nine articles, purification of mothers after childbirth, the surplice and biretta, the use of the wedding ring, the Lord's Prayer, and the laying on of hands. But essential to the observance of these rituals is respect for church government, particularly that of the bishops. In fact, the "Puritans" are primarily characterized as uncontrolled and vulgar in their refusal to accept the principle of hierarchy. For Herbert, the central issue is not theological but social. The view of society that emerges from *Musae Responsoriae* is that of an earthly but sacred harmonious order that works best when people know their proper place and accept their subordination. The Puritans have disrupted this harmony by insisting on an inappropriate leveling of difference and by expecting an impossible purity from flawed mortals. The imagery used to represent the Puritans includes madness, fury, fire, barbarity, rude noise, and body sweat. All of these threaten the harmonious state, because the "vulgar" aims to overthrow the "civilized", the episcopal order.

Melville and the Scottish Presbyterians are criticized in the epigrams for a pride that removes itself from the chain of hierarchical authority: "quits with leaders, quits with teachers" (#5:14).

According to Herbert, the church hierarchy appropriately raises the bishops above others, and thereby cares for the people. The people without a hierarchy are represented as both chaotic and abandoned. In epigram #7, "On the pride of the bishops", Herbert defends the office by defining the episcopacy as a source of divine light:

> Quite often, Mr. Melville,
> You accuse our bishops
> Of puffed up pride.
> Stop it! You are void of shame,
> Or will you call that puffed up which,
> Remote from the people, sticks out
> From paneled ceilings high up?
> So also, buffoon, you would call
> The sun proud, who observes his way
> With so high a globe:
> Yet he, so very high, making
> Fun of what you charge,
> Surrounds the low earth
> With unfailing light. Thus,
> The bishop, as one
> Who has secured high places,
> And who, with his sweet skill,
> Will put a light in those who are
> Unhappy, will have to be applauded.

Like the king, the bishop is compared to the sun, whose high place is understood to be natural and necessary to harmony. James stated his principle of hierarchy in a response to the Millenary Petition: "no bishop, no king". In this poem, hierarchy becomes the means by which divine blessings are distributed to the people. Presbyterians are proud because their attempts to destroy this hierarchy are veiled assertions of self-importance. So epigram #17, "On the bishops":

> Rude evil, sunk in its own ambitions,
> Taunts them [the bishops] now, and since it can't
> Go up those heights itself, rejoices
> To pull them down and sink them to its level.
> O blind people! If the bishop

Is a good thing, why do you deny it?
If evil, better to have of bishops
Very few, than everyone a bishop. (9–16)

The end of the poem reveals Herbert's fear of the leveling effect of
Presbyterianism. "Rude evil" in line 9 is a translation for the phrase
"barbaries impia", more literally, "wickedly undutiful barbarism".
This suggests that the Presbyterians lack civility as well as respect.
For Herbert, the attack on the episcopacy is no new hypothesis,
however wrong, but a regression into a previous, primitive era.

Like the elegies on Prince Henry, the epigrams associate England
with the high civilization and imperial power of the classical world.
Pallas Athena is linked with Cambridge and perhaps again with
England (#6, 37), and Herbert refers to James I as "Caesar" (dedication, #1) and "Augustissime" (most lofty or revered, but also
perhaps a reference to Augustus Caesar, #39:33). Epigram #25 imagines Julius Caesar as he first set foot in Britain; he concludes that the
natives are imminently conquerable since they are naked. Therefore
the Puritan effort to destroy church ceremony is a return to the
primitive:

And so the Puritans,
While they are covetous of a
Lord's bride bare of sacred rites,
And while they wish
All things regressed
To their fathers' barbaric state,
Lay her, entirely
Ignorant of clothing, bare to conquest
By Satan and her enemies. (8–15)

For Herbert, state and church ceremony represent the progress of
the English nation that makes it now parallel to imperial Rome,
rather than to "their fathers' barbaric state". Traditional ceremony,
and the authority and order it represents, arm Britain against its
foes, both spiritual and secular. The Puritans threaten the power
that stems from civilized order through their refusal to obey.

The Puritans are associated with disorder, madness, fire, noise,
and women. "Rude ears" keep them from appreciating sacred music

(#23:45), and their "ungodly noises" interrupt Anglican harmony (#37:22). Scotland burns with an "immodicâ relligione" ["radical religion"], and the flames threaten to destroy the world before the last day (#35:2). Puritan "anger/ disorients all sacred things" ["Cùm sacra perturbet vester furor omnia"] (#3:7). Such "frenzy" turns the Puritan into a bacchante, like the women in Euripides' *Bacchae*, raving outside the bounds of the civilized world: "he then/ Breaks out, and beyond control,/ Wanders in the woods" (#32:9–11; see also #5). Like the women who need to be purified after childbirth because of their responsibility for original sin ("And so the wife, feeling guilty/ For plucking the apple, groans for bearing children", #12:18–19), so the Puritans need to recognize that their inferiority and refusal to accept authority makes them vulnerable to evil and the forces of disorder that threaten the state.

In the epigrams, Herbert makes several references to the Anglican "via media", the middle way between Geneva and Catholic Rome, between no ceremony and too much ceremony, a concept important to his English lyric poems as well (#27, 30, 39:33–37). Yet the poems add to this image of moderation the claim of the preeminence of English civilization over all others: "And Christ himself, watching from the skies,/ Taking in the houses of the world at a glance/ Says that only England offers him a finished worship" (#39:11–13). "Finished worship" is a translation for "plenos ... cultus", more literally, sufficiently full rites. England has reached the end of the civilizing process; other "houses," including Scotland, are unfinished, even at times barbaric. Therefore the beginning of the poem alerts the reader to the potential for an imperial Britain: "Augustissimo Potentissimóque Monarchae Iacobo, D.G. Magnae Britanniae, Franciae, et Hiberniae, Regi, Fidei Defensori" ["To James, Most Venerable and Strongest of Monarchs, by the Grace of God King of Great Britain, France, and Ireland, Defender of the Faith".].

IV. "To the Lady Elizabeth Queen of Bohemia"

Although F.E. Hutchinson placed these verses within the category of "Doubtful Poems" in 1941, Kenneth Alan Hovey and Ted-Larry Pebworth have provided convincing evidence that these two poems are by George Herbert.[27] In them, Herbert expresses his commitment to international Protestantism directly and forcefully.[28] However,

Pebworth and Hovey disagree on the significance of Herbert's author-ship. Pebworth finds that Herbert "does not call the English to arms" but rather instructs Elizabeth to "wait patiently until God deems the time right for her restoration" (113). Hovey however emphasizes that the poems, like "The Church-militant", are "anti-Catholic satires" and "historical-prophetic poems, portraying afflicted good in international conflict with largely Catholic inspired evil and foreseeing the triumph of good and the eventual condemnation of evil" (48). The issue is a significant one: if Herbert is committed to international Protestantism, associated with the military defense of German Protestants in Bohemia and the Palatinate in the Thirty Years' War, how can he also be a pacifist, as so many Herbert critics have claimed?

The first poem is similar to the end of the elegies on Prince Henry, Elizabeth's brother, because both members of the royal family are characterized as most suited to a heavenly rather than an earthly sphere. The "dominions" of Lady Elizabeth are not territorial, but "the sun/ And starrs" as well as her "virtues", now become visible through the self-control she maintains during her grief and loss.[29] The king's daughter, Lady Elizabeth was married in 1613 to the Protestant Frederick, Elector Palatine, who accepted the crown of Bohemia in 1619, but lost it and the Palatinate to Catholic forces in 1621. In the poem, these territories become "two clods of earth", and the affliction of their loss a "black tiffney" mourning scarf, which sets off the "bright" and "transcendent soule" that wears it. From this vantage point, the poem seems to advise renunciation of earthly matters, including war with the Catholic League.

However, the rest of the first poem and the whole of the second prophesy the defeat of "Divell, Jesuit, and Spayne", and the eventual worldwide triumph of the Protestant cause. Certainly it is Elizabeth's children who will triumph, yet they will triumph imperially:

> ... They shall live
> To conquer new ones [kingdoms], and shall share the frame
> Of th'universe, like as the winds, and name
> The world anew. The sunn shall never rise
> But it shall spye some of thy victories.
> Their hands shall clip the eagle's wings and chase
> Those ravening harpies, which peck at their face,

At once to Hell ... (I.42–49)
... Then shall thy glorie, fresh as flowers
In water kept, maugre the powers
Of Divell, Jesuite, and Spayne,
From Holland sayle into the mayne.
Thence, wheeling on, it compasse shall
This, our great sublunarie ball ... (II.7–12)

It is hard to imagine that worldwide conquest will not require some military engagement. This prophecy as well as the reference to Elizabeth's children does emphasize God's control over events rather than immediate action. Nevertheless, when it comes, this action will defeat the eagle of the imperial house, the Austrian Catholic Hapsburgs, as well as the harpies of Spain. The harpies may be another reference to the *Aeneid* by Herbert. The harpies prophesied to Aeneas and his company the long suffering they would experience, but also their eventual destination at Latium, where the history of the Roman Empire would begin (Book III:225–267, 356–395). Thus the sufferings caused by Spain signify the eventual deliverance of "our great sublunarie ball" into the hands of Protestant rulers. One would imagine that at some point arms would have to be used to "conquer" the world (I.43), and rename it (I.44–45).

Critics have largely agreed that Herbert held a personal antipathy to war throughout his life. The evidence for this view stems from two poems in *Lucus*, "In pacem Britannicam" and "Triumphus Mortis", also called "Inventa Bellica", or the invention of war. Critics also cite as evidence Herbert's oration in 1623 before Prince Charles and the Duke of Buckingham advising against war with Spain. I will examine these works later in this chapter. But it would be wise to consider the possibility that Herbert's stance against war may not have been a personally held view, but a politic deference to King James. James was adamant in his refusal to send troops to help his son-in-law Frederick, and continually sought to solve these problems, including the loss of the Palatinate, through mediation and negotiation. James believed that the plans for a marriage between Charles and the Spanish Infanta could end the war of religion on the continent, and usher in an age of peace. Whereas many Protestants advocated immediate war and objected vociferously to the Spanish marriage, George Herbert did not. Yet he shared with these advocates for war the belief that England and the Protestant nations would eventually defeat "Papism" and establish a new religious empire. Herbert's "Church-porch" represents the soldier's life as patriotic, even glorious (87–90). It seems possible that, in hopes of receiving royal patronage, Herbert did not call for war in order to support the king.

V. Latin letters and orations

As Public Orator, Herbert wrote letters for Cambridge that put him in a position to observe the distribution of royal favors rather closely, and he may have been led to hope for his own. We have a record of eighteen Latin letters that he wrote between 1618 and 1621. Although he was elected in January, 1620, a few letters were written before that date, when he was serving as deputy Orator for Francis Nethersole. On January 1, 1618, Herbert wrote a letter of congratulations to the new Marquis of Buckingham. The letter to Buckingham in 1618 displays Herbert's awareness of the favorite's influence over royal patronage: "as rivers which receive waters from a fountain do not themselves retain them, but send them down to the sea; so thou also dost diffuse the dignities derived from our most excellent King over the whole commonwealth."[30] In his official duties, he addressed several others in high office: King James, Chancellor Francis Bacon, Treasurer Lionel Cranfield, Archbishop George Abbot, Bishop Lancelot Andrewes, Secretary of State Robert Naunton, Sir Fulke Greville (457–69). A set of letters dated around January 29, 1621 congratulate many for their promotion to higher office (465–469).

In Herbert's letters to the king, Bohemia and the possibility of war are central issues. Herbert again supports his king's goal of peace, but stresses as well the potential for an English Protestant empire. In a letter dated May 20, 1620, Herbert thanks James for his gift of his Latin works (*Opera Latina*, London, 1619) to the University (458). The letter foresees an imperial triumph through the power of the word rather than the sword, "By this (book) thou dost command the whole world, and dost taste the glory of victory without the cruelty of bloodshed."[31] Herbert opens his letter with a reference to contemporary events: "What! – amid such shakings of the world, hast thou any leisure for us and the Muses?" On August 22, 1619, the Bohemian Estates had deposed their Catholic king Ferdinand and elected Frederick, James's son-in-law. This opened up the possibility that the Protestant princes would have an electoral majority in the German "Holy Roman Empire", presently ruled by the Catholic Hapsburgs. On September 28, 1619, Frederick accepted, despite James's disapproval. The English king made it clear that he would not send money or troops but only help to settle the dispute through mediation.[32] F.E. Hutchinson claims "Herbert's love of peace was in sincere accord with James's pacific policy at a time when most of Europe ... was being drawn into the Thirty Years' War" (604).

But if Hutchinson is right that Herbert had a "love of peace" which was "sincere" rather than a politic recognition of the king's policy, then it was matched with a concern that James rather than a Catholic "command the whole world". James is addressed as moving naturally into an expanded rule:

> Scotland was too narrow for thee to be able fully to unfold thy wings from the nest. What didst thou do thereupon? Thou didst take possession of all the British Isles. Even this empire ["imperium"] was too slender for the vastness of your virtues. So now this book of yours enlarges the bounds, removes the encircling ocean; so that they who are not subject to your power (*ditio*) acknowledge your learning (eru*ditio*).[33]

This goes beyond flattery, since the power of the book resides in its success at defeating Catholicism: "Now we would desire some Jesuit to be given us, that by the sharp application of your book we might crush him then and there." A Jesuit had helped to plan the Gunpowder Plot, and the Jesuits had encouraged the formation of the Catholic League and trained both the Holy Roman Emperor Ferdinand and Maximilian of Bavaria, leaders of the opposition against Frederick and the Protestant Union. Herbert supports the king's pacifism but also brings out his duty as a Protestant prince.

We have only three of Herbert's orations, all given in 1623. However, he refers in his English letters to an oration he will give in Latin in late 1619, and we know he spoke in 1626 on the occasion of Buckingham becoming chancellor of Cambridge (369, xxx). By 1623, the Catholic League had taken Bohemia and had invaded the

Palatinate, and Frederick and Elizabeth were living in The Hague. James again refused to send troops, but hoped to regain the Palatinate through the marriage of Charles and the Spanish Infanta.[34] James had also signaled his frustration with Calvinist and Parliamentary opposition to the Spanish marriage by publishing in August 1622 the "Directions on Preachings", which forbade to all but bishops and deans references in sermons to predestination and Rome. James' stronger patronage for Arminian churchmen can be dated from this point.[35] In February 1623, Charles and Buckingham secretly traveled to Spain to finalize the Spanish marriage. In the same month, Cambridge hosted the ambassadors of the Catholic Habsburg thrones, Spain and Austria. James perhaps leaned on Calvinist Cambridge to declare its support for the king's foreign policy. The proceedings were published "by command", and included Herbert's Latin oration to the ambassadors and an English translation (600).

True Copies of all The Latine Orations, made at Cambridge on the 25. and 27. of Februarie last past [1623] celebrates both the visit of the ambassadors in February and the visit of the king on March 12. The volume describes the arrival of the Austrian ambassador in England, the welcome given to both at Cambridge, the disputations staged, numerous orations given, and the honorary degrees of Master of Arts conferred. It then prints the Vice-Chancellor's speech given in March before the king. Herbert figures prominently in the volume. His oration to the ambassadors is included in Latin and English, and it is described as the "very eloquent Oration" given by "Master *George Herbert*, Orator of that Universitie."[36] The volume ends with Herbert's Latin epigram written for the king's visit, as if it had been chosen as a fit summary of the deference shown by Cambridge to the king's plans for the Spanish marriage.

In an earlier letter requesting help from his stepfather in obtaining the oratorship, Herbert describes the status of the position: "he takes his place next to the Doctors, is at their Assemblies and Meetings, and sits above the Proctors, is Regent or non-Regent at his pleasure, and such like Gaynesses, which will please a young man well" (370). Herbert must have been very pleased at the visit of the king that brought all of Cambridge out in its official clothing and ranks:

The young scholars were placed from Jesus College Gate next the street, into Trinity College Gates in this manner; The Freshmen,

Sophomores, and sophisters all being in their Capps. The Bachelor of Arts in their Hoods and Capps, next to them the Fellow Commoners in their Capps, after them the Regents and non-Regents in their Hoods and Capps. The Proctors, Presidents and Deans of the severall colleges did walk up and down in the streets, to see every one in his degree, to keep his rank and place.[37]

The visit of the Hapsburgs ambassadors did not please all Protestants. Joseph Mede indirectly suggests his horror at the flattery offered to Catholic Spain not just by Herbert but by everyone at Cambridge, "I shall not need to tell you...how our Orators fathered the foundation of our University upon the Spanyards out of the old legend of Cantaber, how happie we were not onely to see them here, but should be to have the Spanish blood come hither." Mede refers to Dr. Beale, the Vice-Chancellor, who claimed that Cambridge was sprung from "a *Spanish Macenas*," and to Herbert, who celebrated the influx of Spanish blood through the marriage of Charles and the Infanta. Herbert uses terms that many Protestants would not have welcomed:

For what could have happened more pleasing to us, then the accesse of the Officers of the Catholicke King? Whose exceeding glory is equally round with the world it selfe: who tying, as with a knot, both *Indias* to his *Spaine*, knows no limits of his praise, no, not, as in past ages, those Pillars of *Hercules*. Long since, all we and our whole Kingdome exult with joy, to bee united with that bloud, which useth to infuse so great and worthie Spirits.[38]

Here Herbert seeks to please King James by flattering his visitors. But all the speeches that day used this kind of excessive praise. In fact it would be a mistake to dismiss Herbert's performance as simple flattery. Herbert's praise for the Catholic Philip IV ("whose exceeding glory is equally round with the world it selfe") echoes the imagined future triumph of the Protestant Lady Elizabeth and her children in Herbert's poems on Bohemia ("Thence, wheeling on, it compasse shall/This, our great sublunarie ball..."). In his oration, Herbert uses the image of the Pillars of Hercules, also used by Bacon on the frontispiece of *Instauratio Magna* (1620) [see Figure 1], to compare the limited progress made by the ancients to the worldwide ambitions of

Figure 1   The frontispiece from Francis Bacon's *Instauratio Magna* (1620), British Library C.54 f.16, by permission of the British Library.

contemporary science and empire. The Public Orator expresses what has recently been called "imperial envy".[39] But he also misrepresents his country's antagonism at mixing English and Spanish "bloud" evident in Parliament and in his own poems. The verses on Bohemia are outspoken in their antipathy to "Divell, Jesuite, and Spayne". "The Church-militant" does not "exult with joy" but laments the influx of Catholic influence into England (235–47). It is interesting that "The Church-militant" names only France and Italy as a source for this pollution. It reserves a special place for Spain, which is characterized as laying down the foundations of empire which the true church will finally occupy, "And where of old the Empire and the Arts/ Usher'd the Gospel ever in mens hearts,/ *Spain* hath done one; when Arts perform the other,/ The Church shall come ..." (263–266). It is possible that Herbert truly believed that James's pacifism and alliance with Spain would make possible a worldwide conversion to Protestantism through "arts" rather than arms. Yet it is difficult to believe that Herbert would "exult with joy" over a Catholic queen in England. This wording in his oration to the Spanish ambassadors as well as his views about peace in general may have been strategic rather than sincere.

King James seems to have taken a liking to Herbert during this time. Walton claims that the king noticed and commented on Herbert's letter and epigram of May 20, 1620. Nevertheless the only contemporary evidence suggests that it was actually Herbert's oration to the ambassadors on February 27, 1623, and the short farewell oration and epigram given to the king on March 12, 1623, that attracted the king's attention. Hutchinson cites this account of James's visit to Cambridge on March 12 in which the king reads Herbert's epigram: "Dr. Richardson, Master of Trinity, 'brought before the King a paper of verses in manner of a Epigram which B[ishop] Neale & others read.'" (598). It is interesting that both Richardson and Neile were Arminians. Hutchinson also includes another account, "After refreshments, they brought the king 'to the door, entering into the Court, where his Coach did wait for him: but his Majesty was pleased to stay there, while the Orator Mr. Herbert did make a short Farewell Speech unto him. Then he called for a copy of the Vice-Chancellor's Speech, & likewise for an Epigram the Orator made'" (600). The farewell oration Herbert gave that day is a very short, playful set of compliments about how

James's innumerable virtues could never be fully articulated. Nevertheless the Orator is serious in his emphasis on James's role as defender of the faith, and Herbert cites again James's ability to defeat the Jesuits in his writings. However, Herbert's epigram is sheer flattery:

> Dum petit Infantem Princeps, Grantámque Iacobus,
> Quisnam horum maior sit, dubitatur, amor.
> Vincit more suo Noster: nam millibus Infans
> Non tot abest, quot nos Regis ab ingenio.

> ["While Prince to Spaine, and King to Cambridge goes,
> The question is, whose love the greater showes:
> Ours (like himselfe) o'ercomes; for his wit's more
> Remote from ours, then Spaine from Britains shoare."] (437–8)

The publication of this epigram at the end of the volume *True Copies of all the Latine Orations* sums up the deference shown to the king at Cambridge, and suggests that the king did indeed see Herbert as a spokesman for royal policy at this time. Herbert also seems to be negotiating well the king's shift towards Arminianism that began the year before. In the account quoted above, the Arminian Dr. Richardson, Master of Herbert's College Trinity, chooses to display Herbert's epigram to the king and the Arminian Bishop Neile, who may have remembered Herbert from Westminster School.

Traditionally it has been assumed that Herbert's opportunities for royal favor evaporated with his oration on October 8, 1623 to Prince Charles and the new Duke of Buckingham. The two had returned from Spain after learning that the Pope's conditions for the marriage were tolerance for public worship for English Catholics as well as the conversion to Catholicism of Prince Charles and Frederick's heir.[40] Herbert's speech included gratitude for the prince's return, the traditionally excessive compliments, and a strong argument against war. Critics have concluded that, since both Charles and Buckingham came home ready for war with Spain, Herbert destroyed his chances for promotion by expressing his personal anti-war views.[41] Charles became king in 1625, and Buckingham continued to dispense royal patronage.

But this conclusion needs to be reconsidered and modified for a variety of reasons. Jeffrey Powers-Beck has shown that, whereas Buckingham was quite explicit in his desire for war by October 1623, Charles had not yet made his views known.[42] Mede's comments on the day demonstrate that he and his friends at Cambridge had no definite knowledge of the future of the marriage: "We have nothing of the match at all, but we are sure yet the Infanta is not come."[43] In fact, Charles was still pursuing the marriage to the Infanta, but under the condition that the Palatinate be restored to his brother-in-law Frederick before the marriage took place.[44] Charles did not give up his hopes until late November. King James was still adamant in his opposition to war. The publication of the oration in 1623 was another announcement of Herbert's support for the king's policies. In addition, one of George Herbert's most important patrons, William Herbert, the earl of Pembroke, was backing the king against Buckingham. Rather than explicitly disagreeing with the prince and duke, George Herbert sided with the king and Pembroke against Buckingham. I have suggested elsewhere that George probably spoke for Pembroke at this point, as Benjamin Rudyerd spoke for Pembroke in the House of Commons. It may be that George's reward was his position as M.P. the next year in a seat under the purview of Pembroke.[45]

Although Herbert's comments against war are forceful, they take up only three of the twenty pages of the speech.[46] Throughout, the emphasis is on support for the policies of King James. Herbert expresses the gratitude of the English at Charles' safe return, and perhaps relief that the Spanish marriage did not take place, but Herbert concludes that the prince's marriage will be arranged, "according to the judgment of a king most wise and most experienced in things human and divine" (398). The son's original pursuit of the marriage was motivated, according to Herbert, by the pacifism of his father, "And in this marriage our most sweet prince not only had a view to posterity, but also to the present age, while he desires the peace which we freely enjoy now for so many years in this way to be secured and everlasting; and where in the world may this be hoped for if not from the Spaniard?" (405). In the speech, Herbert in fact does not rule out war, but approves it only if the king leads the way, "But it is not our duty to proclaim war; our most prudent king will timely foresee where he should lift up the standard; the British lions ... which now are gentle, will roar sufficiently" (406). "... The same force which traversed Spain will, if need be, conquer it ..." (414). Herbert's "vehement indictment of war", as Hutchinson put it, apparently would yield to James's command. Herbert chides the English for worries over the Spanish marriage since they display a distrust of the king's policies, "I know that the Spaniard is clever, skillful, very knowing in art and craft; but James is on our side" (410). The principle of the speech is not aversion to war but support for James. It is unlikely that Herbert would have alienated Charles with this message, since Charles at the time was pursuing the same course: the restoration of the Palatinate to Frederick through the Spanish marriage rather than war.

Although the oration advocates obedience to the king rather than opposition to war, it may nevertheless have damaged Herbert's career. The prince is warmly praised, but Herbert never mentions Buckingham once. Herbert seems to have drastically miscalculated by under-estimating Buckingham's influence over Charles. Also, it is possible that Herbert erred in his tone, since he frequently preaches to the prince as if he were a younger brother (Charles was 23; Herbert 30). Finally, Buckingham may have excluded Herbert as a possible client because of Pembroke's patronage, since, in the following years, Buckingham came to see Pembroke as a dangerous enemy.

VI. *Passio Discerpta* and *Lucus*

The best treatment of these two collections of Latin epigrams is by W. Hilton Kelliher in "The Latin Poetry of George Herbert".[47] Kelliher demonstrates that, given epigrams XXV–XXVIII in *Lucus*, the final version of the collections must have been compiled after August 1623 when Cardinal Maffeo Barbarini became Pope Urban VIII. According to Kelliher, *Passio Discerpta* is part of a tradition of neo-Latin sacred epigram written also by Richard Crashaw and the continental Jesuit Jacob Bidermann, and is influenced as well by secular Latin epigrams published by Thomas Campion and John Owen. Also central to the work is the practice of meditation advocated by Catholics and Protestants on the life of Christ, specifically the events of the passion. Kelliher shows that witty correspondences between events in the Bible, ingenious conceits, and the focus on paradox characterize the poems.

The set of epigrams is also illuminating about Herbert's best-known work *The Temple*. Kelliher believes that the tension and drama important to the lyrics of *The Temple* are replaced in the Latin verses by wit and paradox. Nevertheless the events of the passion had a special significance for Herbert, since his birthday at times fell on the same day as Good Friday, and he uses Good Friday as the setting for the beginning of "The Church" in *The Temple*. Herbert explores this significance in another Latin poem "In Natales et Pascha Concurrentes" ["On the concurrence of a birthday and Good Friday"], probably written in 1618.[48] Like the colloquy in the practice of meditation, *Passio Discerpta* draws out the meaning of events of Christ's passion for the individual, and, in doing so, the collection lays the groundwork for the opening of "The Church".

Lucus differs from *Passio Discerpta* because it combines epigrams of religious thought with those of moral teaching. Both collections consider the issue of the altar internalized in the hard heart, so fundamental to Herbert's notion of religious poetry and also his method of reconciling Puritan inwardness with Anglican ceremony (*Passio Discerpta* 19, 20; *Lucus* 1, 29). But *Lucus* takes up as well moral behavior within society, and considers several sins associated with misguided social choices: pride, vainglory, avarice, gluttony, and wrath. For Herbert in *Lucus*, and, we will see later, in *The Temple*, religious grace and the altar of the heart are not associated with a purely religious life but make themselves visible in self-disciplined social action. "On vainglory" considers a problem important to Herbert as he became more prominent at Cambridge. He does not condemn the pursuit of glory in itself, but only its excesses:

> Don't let your fame be loose, don't suck it in too much;
> Be moderate in what you do. If glory
> Leads the column, rein it in; if it
> Lags behind, let it loose.
> Moroseness has a curdlike thickness,
> And giddiness is rennet-thin. (15–20)[49]

Inner balance would have been important to Herbert as he gained public recognition. We have seen that he was receiving the notice of King James by 1623. *Lucus* includes evidence that Herbert's epigram on Roma as an anagram had been answered by the Pope. According to Kelliher, *Lucus* prints the epigram on Roma (XXV) preceding Pope Urbanus VIII's answer, as well as two counter-responses by Herbert. Kelliher argues that the epigram on Roma had been originally part of *Musae Responsoriae*, but had circulated independently, since Cardinal Maffeo Barbarini, Pope Urbanus in 1623, had seen it, and answered it in his own epigram.[50] By including the epigrams in succession in *Lucus*, Herbert announces his role as a Protestant apologist, but also as a poet receiving international attention. More evidence for this developing reputation is provided by epigram XXXII, "Triumphus Mortis", which in its original form as "Inventa Bellica", has survived in two manuscripts, and may have been written to complement the work of Thomas Reid, the king's Latin Secretary from 1618–1624.[51]

Like epigram VI "On the British Peace", "The Triumph of Death" supports James's pacific policy. The first is a short poem praising England as an island surrounded by walls of water, which protect it from the bloodshed felt by other European nations in the Thirty Years' War. The second poem is a long meditation on the role of death in human civilization, beginning with Cain and Abel, moving to the professional soldier, and ending with both the invention of gunpowder and Jesuits who plan the assassination of monarchs, a reference to Father Henry Garnett and the Gunpowder Plot. The poem is imaginative and passionate in its condemnation of "violence's dark hyena". Nevertheless the traditional claim that the poem represents Herbert's personal beliefs needs to be weighed against the evidence that King James noticed Herbert in 1623 particularly for an oration and epigram that supported the king's pacifism and plans for a Spanish marriage. This suggests that the anti-war poems in *Lucus*, like the oration to Charles and Buckingham on October 6, 1623, primarily supported the position of the king. Herbert's anti-Catholicism remains the same, since the Pope is named the Antichrist (X). The ancient Roman empire remains the high-point of civilization:

> *Rome*, what *frontier* did your name
> Not cross, when times of old endured
> The Latin yoke? Fame you did not lack,
> Nor songs of fame, when *Maro*
> Made you eminent among the stars. (XXV: 1–4)[52]

It is remarkable how often Herbert refers to P. Vergilius Maro in his university works. Herbert and Virgil seem an unlikely pair, but only because our image of Herbert as the gentle poet of Bemerton obscures from view his imperial hopes for his Protestant nation, frequently expressed in the poetry of the period. This chapter has demonstrated that, whereas King James never seems to have provided Herbert with any sort of position, the king did recognize Herbert as a defender of foreign policy with Spain, since Herbert's oration and epigram on these matters were published "by command". Herbert's hopes of royal patronage may have been even stronger, given his brother Henry's success in this regard. Henry became the king's servant after being introduced by William Herbert, earl of Pembroke, in 1622. Henry was knighted by the king and made Master of the Revels in August 1623, just three months before George Herbert's oration before Charles and Buckingham. Therefore, George Herbert in concert with Pembroke may have seen the oration as an opportunity to defend the king's foreign policy. The poems against war in *Lucus*, written some time after August 1623, were perhaps an opportunity to play Virgil to James's Augustus.

3
1624 and *The Temple*

The Temple should be considered within the context of the events of 1624. I hope to show that the poetic sequence is evidence for Herbert's engagement in the world during this year and through-out his life. *The Temple* displays Herbert's effort, most visible to modern readers in the events of 1624, to link together a deep spiritual devotion, ethical behavior, professional activities, and a commitment to the future of world Protestantism. Although the lyrics in *The Temple* have been approached as evidence of Herbert's meditative withdrawal from worldly events, I will argue, as have many others, that these lyrics should be considered in the context of contemporary events, and in terms of the rest of the work, including "The Church-porch", and "The Church-militant". The following chapter will substantiate this argument through a consideration of the events of 1624 and the parts of *The Temple*, including "The Dedication", "The Church-porch", "The Church", and "The Church-militant". The chapter will end with a summary of the various explanations for the structure of *The Temple*.[1]

I. The events of 1624

1624 was a critical year for George Herbert. He attended parliament for the first and only time. He delayed the ordination expected of Cambridge fellows 20 months past the limit required in the University statutes. He witnessed Prince Charles, the Duke of Buckingham, and parliament work against the policies of King

53

James, and move the country toward war with Spain. Finally in November, Herbert asked to be ordained as a deacon immediately, rather than wait the usual year. Ordination as a deacon meant that he was a member of the clergy, although he could not yet serve as a priest, that he could no longer attend parliament, and that many secular positions would not be open to him.[2] What led him to make this sudden move?

Various theories have been offered. Walton claimed that Herbert had to give up his "court hopes" because his primary patrons had died, including King James. According to this view, Herbert subsequently retreated from competition for patronage into humble obedience to the established church. However Walton did not realize that Herbert had requested ordination in 1624, before the death of the king. Amy Charles, who discovered this detail, believed that Herbert was aiming at the ministry from the outset, and that parliament was simply a temporary detour. However, Diana Benet has argued that, in the parliament of 1624, Herbert witnessed the power of Buckingham and the weakness of King James in the patronage of court officials, and that Herbert consequently took up the ministry as his career: "Regardless of his spiritual inclinations, Herbert's abandonment of court hopes could have been dictated by practical considerations alone."[3]

The death of King James probably did matter very much to Herbert, but not for the reasons that Walton gives. Herbert may have delayed his ordination because of the attention he received from King James in February and March of 1623. According to the statute of Cambridge University on the ordination of its fellows, Herbert should have taken orders in March 1623.[4] But around that time, Herbert presented an oration to the Spanish ambassadors and epigram to the king that were published in 1623 as support for James' Spanish policy (see Chapter 2). His brother Henry was appointed as Master of the Revels in August 1623, and George may have expected a similar appointment, perhaps as apologist for James. The publication after October 1623 of Herbert's oration to Charles and Buckingham also announced Herbert's support for the king, and also, perhaps, the influence of Herbert's actual patron, William Herbert, Earl of Pembroke. However, the new power acquired by Prince Charles and the

Duke of Buckingham by 1624, as well as their antagonism to a Spanish marriage, would have undermined Herbert's plans to seek preferment from the king as a defender of his foreign policy. But there is no reason to believe that Herbert was counting out promotion to high office all together. Given his career up to this point, it is more reasonable to assume that he expected to be appointed to a promising church position by any number of patrons, including the king or Pembroke, or to a significant secular position open to a deacon. The best way to accomplish this would be to avoid parliament's disputes with the king, as well as its factionalism.

With the guidance of Prince Charles and the Duke of Buckingham, the 1624 houses of parliament continually challenged and defied King James' pacifist program as well as his belief that parliament should not interfere with foreign policy. By the end of the session, James had conceded that he would be advised but not ruled by parliament. The king agreed to break the treaties with Spain, and wage war on the continent for the return of the Palatinate. However he would not agree to attack Spain directly. Buckingham sought industriously to bring king and parliament together, but he also began negotiations with France for a marriage between the prince and Henrietta Maria, the conditions of which were largely kept secret. Between September and December of 1624, tensions developed between the Privy Council and the prince and duke, who were keeping the councilors out of the negotiations. Friction was particularly strong between Buckingham and Pembroke: the duke prevented Pembroke and Arundel from becoming dukes, and excluded them and nearly all the privy councilors from signing the marriage treaty with France in December 1624.[5]

In this climate of suspicion, George Herbert may have concluded that the next session of parliament would be even more combative than the last. The 1624 parliament was scheduled to resume around Michaelmas, September 29, but it was delayed until February 26, 1625.[6] As a client of Pembroke, Herbert would probably have voted for war against the king's pacific policy in the 1624 session, and would be expected to oppose the foreign policy of King James and support any investigation into Buckingham's actions in 1625. Ordination in November 1624 would protect Herbert from factional conflict and from voting against the interests of the king. Although the king died before the next session, the 1625 parliament lived up to these expectations: the Commons began to investigate Buckingham's actions, and the session was abruptly dissolved. Buckingham suspected that the privy councilors were responsible, including Pembroke, and the duke was probably correct. In 1626, Pembroke seems to have led the fight to impeach Buckingham.[7]

Parliament was becoming uncomfortably heated for other reasons. In 1624, Herbert served on a committee that considered charges against his master at Trinity, the Arminian John Richardson. Although the charges were dropped, perhaps through Herbert's efforts, parliament began directly attacking Arminianism in this session. Herbert would have agreed with this theologically but not strategically, if he still held hopes of patronage from the king. James had been more supportive to Arminians since mid-1622. Buckingham and Charles had not yet announced their preference for Arminianism, made evident only in 1626. In 1623, Herbert seems to be successfully negotiating James' shift toward Arminianism partly through his relationship to Richardson [see Ch.2], but would have felt a strong conflict of interest in parliamentary debates.[8]

During the 1624 session, the members of the Virginia Company also spoke in opposition to the king, who was ready to dissolve their business, and who refused to allow the issue to be considered in the Commons. Nicholas Ferrar defended the company at the time, but it was later said of him, "For these engagements and his too free speeches against the will of his prince, though exceedingly well meant, were so deep and so long a regret and shame to him afterwards, that he was heard to say, (stretching out his right hand), *I would I were assured of the pardon of that sin, though on that condition this right hand were cut off.*" I am not attributing to Herbert a similar conscience-stricken patriotism, but rather a strategic effort to avoid opposing the king in parliament in order to keep open the possibility of royal preferment to a position within the church.[9]

By considering *The Temple* in the context of 1624, I hope to show that the issues significant to Herbert during that year are also significant to *The Temple*: the problems of Arminianism and

Puritanism, the importance and difficulties of a Protestant empire, and his own pursuit of patronage and employment.

II. "The Dedication"

"The Dedication" repeats similar poems in *Musae Responsoriae* but focuses on God as the sole source for inspiration rather than a human patron:

> *Lord, my first fruits present themselves to thee;*
> *Yet not mine neither: for from thee they came,*
> *And must return. Accept of them and me,*
> *And make us strive, who shall sing best thy name.*
> *Turn their eyes hither, who shall make a gain:*
> *Theirs, who shall hurt themselves or me, refrain.*

As Michael Schoenfeldt has established, the language used here originated in secular dedications that conventionally described patrons as the source of the value of the text.[10] Herbert had hinted at the same issue in *Musae Responsoriae* through his reference to the Nile in his poems to the king and to God (see Ch. 2). "First fruits" (1) refer to the first of the agricultural harvest, often offered to God or the gods, and to payments, usually the amount of the first year's income, paid to a superior by each new holder of a ecclesiastical benefice or any office. The language of patronage determines Herbert's dedication, but this also suggests that throughout the poet's search for employment Herbert used *The Temple* to remind himself of his duty to God.[11] Rather than a renunciation of the pursuit of patronage, then, *The Temple* requires that it proceed with an awareness of God's ultimate authority and power. In *Musae* (1620–1), the penultimate poem "To His Serene Majesty" is followed by "To God", which concludes "Quod scribo, & placeo, si placeo, tuum est." [What I write and how I please, if I please, belongs to you].[12] Schoenfeldt is right that the strategic deference used by clients to flatter their patrons shapes Herbert's devotion, but this devotion is also intended to ground Herbert's pursuit of patronage on a spiritual basis. The end of the "Dedication" suggests that divine patronage can best ensure the successful future of the book and protect the writer from unfriendly readers.

III. "The Church-porch"

It is conventional to describe "The Church-porch" as a set of moral aphorisms that prepare the reader for the deeper spiritual mysteries of "The Church". The subtitle "Perirrhanterium" refers to an instrument used in sprinkling holy water. This emphasizes church ceremony, but also suggests that the moral precepts in "The Church-porch" rather than any physical ritual are the best preparation for deeper religious matters.[13] The church porch was associated with schooling, and also with settling money transactions, paying dowries, rents, and purchases of estates.[14] Just as a church is entered through the porch, and just as the school sometimes located in that porch or in a room over it guides young men toward adulthood, so the ethics of "The Church-porch" lead the reader to a mature spirituality. Precepts on sexuality, drinking, oaths, gambling, quarreling, clothes, and behavior in church teach self-discipline and good manners. The opening lines addressed to a "sweet youth" and the admonition against "dressing, mistressing, and complement" (80) suggest that part of the plan is to steer the sons of the gentry toward the ministry, as Donne does in "To Mr. Tilman, Taking Orders."

However the ministry is never mentioned, whereas Herbert's primary target is the general "idlenesse" of the English upper classes (79–96). The work gives instructions on how to prepare for a variety of occupations, including local government, scholarship, the military, and the maintenance of an upper-class estate (79–120). Despite Herbert's anti-war arguments made for the king, the soldier's life is presented as patriotic, even glorious (90). Therefore the morality taught by the work includes dedication to professional activities, not as a superficial, worldly distraction, but as a religious and nationalistic duty: "O England! full of sinne, but most of sloth;/ Spit out thy flegme, and fill thy brest with glorie" (91–2).

The reference to idleness demonstrates Herbert's interest in the Protestant ethic, or, as it was called at the time, the doctrine of vocation. Formulated first by Luther and developed by William Perkins and other English preachers, the doctrine taught that the highest form of spirituality in the world was not the monastic life but labor in a calling. Perkins organized vocation into two parts: the general calling, by which God called the soul to conversion and election, and the particular calling, or one's social estate or profession. Therefore "The Church-porch" is linked to "The Church" not only in terms of time, as in a movement from youth to maturity, but also in terms of space, as suggested by the architectural metaphor. The individual's dedication to a particular social estate or profession is accompanied by the drama of salvation that goes on within the soul.[15]

Herbert addresses the idle heir to a landed estate, and preaches education, religious training, and financial prudence (91–115, 103–204). However, he seems most interested in the younger son of the gentry, like himself, who is dependent on an occupation for his income. The "stock" (300, 346) of this man is not in bloodlines, property, money, or herds, but in the "credit" (346) or reputation that must be developed and protected most carefully for the sake of eventual preferment. Pleasing others is a delicate but required duty (289, 296, 326). Although "worth and service" as well as "substantial worth" are praised rather than clothes or boldness in manner, nevertheless "conversation" is of primary importance. Rules are provided on the proper use of wit, modes of addressing the great, the best way to please one's auditors, and the advantages of calmness in argument (205–256, 289–324). Moreover, Herbert advocates a temperate, but continual "business": "A grain of glorie mixt with humblenesse/ Cures both a fever and lethargicknesse./...Let thy mind still be bent, still plotting where,/ And when, and how the business may be done" (335–8).

Several critics have argued that "The Church-porch" was written early in Herbert's University career, and that it displays an interest in promotion that he later renounced after entering the ministry.[16] However, at the time, preferment was as much a concern in the ministry as in any other profession. Instead of assuming that Herbert matured spiritually beyond the school-precepts of "The Church-porch", it is worth considering that these rules may have represented his own practice in pursuing patronage throughout his life, during his University years, in the 1624 parliament, and afterwards, in seeking advancement within the church.

IV. "The Church"

This group of lyrics, the most famous of Herbert's works, shows evidence of authorial planning particularly at the beginning and end. It is clear from the two available manuscripts of Herbert's *Temple* that the first and last set of poems in "The Church" were constructed early in the process, and that the structure was developed to allow for the addition of individual poems in the middle of the sequence. [17] Although revised to some extent, the opening poems in both manuscripts represent the speaker as meditating on the events of Good Friday before turning to a consideration of Easter and baptism. This evokes the period around Easter when initiates were accepted as members in the church and baptized. The closing sequence represents the speaker meditating on "last things", on death, final judgment, and heaven. Thus "The Church" follows out the life of a Christian, perhaps that of Herbert, although the traces of autobiography are indirect and difficult to follow. Throughout, Herbert comments on contemporary controversies about theology and liturgy.

Directly before "The Church", the "Superliminare" marks the transition from secular to sacred. The word is used in the Vulgate Bible in Exodus 12:22 to describe the sign of blood the Israelites put on the lintel to preserve themselves from God's punishment of the Egyptians. The first verse of the "Superliminare" welcomes those who have learned "how to behave" themselves in church from the moral precepts of "The Church-porch", but the second makes a much more severe religious distinction, excluding the profane, perhaps the pagan or the unelect, but also suggesting that even the godly elite will be deeply challenged within:

> Thou, whom the former precepts have
> Sprinkled and taught, how to behave
> Thy self in church; approach, and taste
> The churches mysticall repast.
>
> Avoid, Profaneness; come not here:
> Nothing but holy, pure, and cleare,
> Or that which groneth to be so,
> May at his perill further go.

"At his perill" refers both to those who are "holy, pure, and cleare" as well as those who "groneth to be so"; the process of grace requires the risk of self-examination throughout one's life.[18]

The lyrics within offer the "the churches mysticall repast" ("Superliminare", 4), as they carry on the work of *Musae Responsoriae* by representing conformist Calvinism as the "middle way" between Puritanism and Catholicism.[19] Herbert takes a stand on certain theological issues, particularly predestination and grace, but he also seems interested in providing opportunities for agreement between the opposing parties. The "sacred ritual" of the Church of England is celebrated, just as it would be by Arminians, but not for their reasons or those of Catholics. Both of these groups would consider ritual as a means to obtain merit for salvation or a sign of obedience to authority. Rather, Herbert emphasizes the Calvinist view that salvation can be acquired by grace alone. As in *Lucus* and *Passio Discerpta*, Herbert takes up the formal aspects of the church to show that church liturgy becomes spiritually significant when grace internalizes it within the worshipper. "Reasonable sacrifice" from *Lucus* clarifies this point:

> If one considers the rise of men and altars,
> Earth breathed upon was man, dead earth
> An altar. These, which separated
> From one another make for harm, through Christ's compacts
> Were put together: so man becomes
> The living altar of God.[20]

Why do men and altars "separated/ From one another make for harm" in Herbert's view? Herbert clarifies in *"The Country Parson"* that he believes there is "no holiness in the things" of church furniture (246). The opening sequence of "The Church" implies that altars alone are idolatrous because the Catholic mass gives a false authority to priest and church by claiming to reproduce the sacrifice of Christ, and because the Arminians emphasize obedience to authority without regard for inner devotion. However, men without altars are like the Puritans, who replace the church's authority with their own, and follow their subjective responses rather than the authority of "sacred ritual". Becoming "the living altar of God" is a "reasonable sacrifice" because it respects the authority of the church, and it acknowledges that the excessive emphasis on the physical altar characteristic of the Arminians actually leave the real matter untouched: internal reformation through "Christ's compacts", the grace obtained through the crucifixion. This view underlies the first poem of "The Church":

The Altar.

A broken A L T A R, Lord, thy servant reares;
Made of a heart, and cemented with tears:
   Whose parts are as thy hand did frame;
   No workmans tool hath touch'd the same.
      A H E A R T alone
      Is such a stone,
      As nothing but
      Thy pow'r doth cut.
      Wherefore each part
      Of my hard heart
      Meets in this frame,
      To praise thy Name:
   That, if I chance to hold my peace,
   These stones to praise thee may not cease.
O, let thy blessed S A C R I F I C E be mine,
And sanctifie this A L T A R to be thine.

In 1617, the Arminians in Durham Cathedral took the wooden communion table symbolizing the Last Supper out of its position in the choir placed east-west and placed it north-south altar-wise at the east end of the chancel. Around 1620, the communion table in the cathedral was replaced entirely with a stone altar.[21] In 1634, after Herbert's death, Charles and Laud tried to replace all communion tables with altars, and Herbert's patron John Williams, Bishop of Lincoln, opposed Laud in the work *The Holy Table, Name and Thing.*[22] Herbert's poetic altar claims indirectly that the Arminians have separated men from altars, since they focus only on ceremony and obedience to external authority rather than the grace needed for internal reformation. However Herbert also seems to be forging an image that can illuminate what is true in the approach of each group. Puritans would appreciate the emphasis on grace, Arminians the reverence implicit in the use of the altar, and conforming Calvinists, those most like Herbert, would value his ability to unite internal regeneration with external forms. Although it might seem that Herbert endorses the Arminian replacement of the communion table with the altar, in fact he demonstrates that altars become significant when they are internalized, and such reformation can only occur through the power of grace rather than works:

> A HEART alone
> Is such a stone,
> As nothing but
> Thy pow'r doth cut.

"Thy power" cuts through the hardness of the heart through grace, whereas human efforts have a much more limited effect, like a poet cutting poetic lines from four feet to two. Stanley Fish and others have demonstrated that "The Altar" works on a contrast between human and divine works. The poem represents "thy servant" as rearing the altar in the heart and on the page (1–2), but God is described as framing its parts (3–4). For a moment, God seems to write the poem.[23] Grace rather than merit breaks the resistance within and provides the willingness to obey. This emphasis on grace is quite different from the Arminian insistence on obedience to church authority. For Herbert, God's grace alone makes one willing to obey. This willingness brings together the heart in a new form, memorialized on the page as a poem of praise in the shape of an altar, which, like Shakespeare's sonnets, will last through time (13–14). The final couplet acknowledges the power of Christ's sacrifice, as well as its ability to bring the speaker from this position of willingness, with his resistance broken, to complete sanctification (16), where all parts of the heart will yield to grace.

Critics disagree on whether or not Herbert's poetic altar is a finished product, representing the speaker's reception of grace, or "broken" in poetic and spiritual ways.[24] Some point to the fact that the altar is an extremely elaborate work of art and appears in the problematic shape of an "I". Certainly from 1610 Herbert associated the image of the altar with the dedication of his poetic powers to God. Therefore he could be considering here as he does in many other poems the purity of motive behind such a dedication.[25] The remaining hardness of the heart may be evident in the speaker's eagerness to reproduce the sacrifice of Christ as his own (15), since the poem has questioned from the outset the value of merit and personal achievement in the process of salvation. *The Book of Common Prayer* includes the following prayer after communion: "And here we offer and present unto thee, O Lord, ourselves, our souls and bodies, to be a reasonable, holy, and lively sacrifice unto thee." But the speaker's desire in line 15 of "The Altar" verges on an unreasonable sacrifice, since he moves beyond acknowledging the power of grace to the desire to imitate Christ. *The Book of Common Prayer* is more moderate in its claims: "although we be unworthy, through our manifold sins, to offer unto thee any sacrifice, yet we beseech thee to accept this our bounden duty and service; not weighing our merits, but pardoning our offences through Jesus Christ our Lord."[26]

This issue becomes explicit in the next poem "The Sacrifice". Spoken from the point of view of Christ on the cross, the poem uses irony to clarify the absolute difference between a human and a divine point of view. Those responsible for the crucifixion are exposed as utterly ignorant of the significance of the event. The poem proclaims the fallacy of the Catholic view that this sacrifice ("a full, perfect, and sufficient sacrifice") could be repeated during the mass, and the poem may also suggest the inadequacy of the speaker's view that his sacrifice could reproduce that of Christ: [27]

> *Oh all ye, who passe by*, whose eyes and minde
> To worldly things are sharp, but to me blinde;
> To me, who took eyes that I might you finde:
> > Was ever grief like mine? (1–4)

The poem is unique amongst the lyrics in "The Temple" for two reasons. It is based on the Catholic liturgy of the reproaches, or *Improperia*, Christ's complaints about the people on Good Friday, and it is the only poem in which God or Christ is the speaker throughout. It also marks a transition not only from the Old to the New Testament, but also from Catholicism to Protestantism, since the theme of the opening sequence after "The Sacrifice" is the inability of the speaker to imitate Christ's sacrifice.[28] In fact, the speaker uses his seemingly righteous desire to imitate Christ as a distraction from his real religious need: an acknowledgment of the suffering and power of the crucifixion. "The Sacrifice" makes the crucifixion difficult to ignore:

> *Pilate*, a stranger, holdeth off; but they,
> Mine own deare people, cry, *Away, away,*
> With noises confused frighting the day:
>   Was ever grief like mine?

> Yet still they shout, and crie, and stop their eares,
> Putting my life among their sinnes and fears,
> And therefore wish *my bloud on them and theirs*:
>   Was ever grief like mine?

> See how spite cankers things. These words aright
> Used, and wished, are the whole worlds light:
> But hony is their gall, brightnesse their night:
>   Was ever grief like mine? (101–112)

As Pilate considers freeing Jesus, the Jews call out for his condemnation. Christ's grief stems from the hate of "mine own dear people", as well as from the irony implicit in the phrase "my bloud on them and theirs". The Jews take responsibility for the death of Jesus, since Pilate will not, but Christ recognizes that, properly meant, these words could provide eternal salvation for his people. Christ's blood means two things at once: the torture of hate and pain that results in his death, and the redemptive grace that this sacrifice provides for those able to receive it.

The salvation imagined is both individual and global. As the verses above put it "These words aright/ Used, and wished, are the whole worlds light" (109–110). Few commentators notice that the poem considers the possibility of the conversion of the Jews as well as the world-wide salvation hoped for by European Protestants, and described by Herbert in "The Church-militant": "These drops being temper'd with a sinners tears,/ A Balsome are for both the Hemispheres" ("The Sacrifice", 25–6). According to commentator John Tobin, these hemispheres refer to east and west: "given that *The Temple* ultimately speaks of religion moving westward and to America".[29] Therefore the confrontation between the speaker and Christ's passion that occurs in the opening sequence will make possible not only speaker's entrance into the church, but also his participation in its militant activities.

First, however, he needs to give up his misguided effort to match Christ's sacrifice with his own. In "The Thanksgiving", this urge is revealed to be a form of competition by which he avoids facing the power of grace:

> But how then shall I imitate thee, and
>   Copie thy fair, though bloudie hand? ...
> Then for thy passion – I will do for that –
>   Alas, my God, I know not what. (15–6, 49–50).

In "George Herbert – The Giver and the Gift", William Nestrick demonstrates that the speaker in "The Thanksgiving" finally has to recognize that he is unable to offer anything comparable to Christ's sacrifice.[30] These attempts at giving include a full-fledged art of poetry modeled on Christ's love, which sounds a great deal like the "sacred parody" in *The Temple* itself (39–48). The speaker's competitive gift-giving, including that represented by the title, obscures from his own view the inadequacy of his attempts to prove his merit, as well as his full dependence on grace. The Calvinism implicit in the poem is underscored by the poem's reference to predestination (31), a doctrine that the Arminians refuted, King James in August 1622 urged preachers not to mention, and King Charles ruled out of order in June 1626.[31] Herbert opposes this position through his "poetry of grace", which continues in "The Reprisal". This title refers to musical refrain and military retaliation, and the poem spells out the terms of the speaker's competition with Christ. By the end of the poem, however the speaker finally capitulates:

> O make me innocent, that I
> May give a disentangled state and free:
> And yet thy wounds still my attempts defie,
>   For by thy death I die for thee ...
>
> Yet by confession will I come
> Into thy conquest: though I can do nought
> Against thee, in thee I will overcome
>   The man, who once against thee fought. (5–8, 13–16)

The opening sequence then settles into a pattern of self-examination and confession, urged by the church before taking communion and integral to the process of becoming a member during Easter. The poem "Easter-wings" once more uses the tradition of the pattern-poem with which the sequence began in "The Altar". Now the speaker remembers the importance of grace throughout:

> Lord, who createdst man in wealth and store,
>   Though foolishly he lost the same,
>   Decaying more and more
>   Till he became
>   Most poore:
>   With thee
>   O let me rise
>   As larks, harmoniously,
>   And sing this day thy victories:
> Then shall the fall further the flight in me. (1–10)

This poem recognizes the effect of the fall and original sin as both historical fact and personal reality. The harmonious shape of the poem represents the effect of yielding to Christ's grace, and acting not in competition, but "with thee" (6), just as "The Reprisal" calls on the speaker not to work "against thee" but "in thee" (15). Although "The Altar" focuses on grace from the third line, it never quite escapes the problems associated with hardness of the heart. "Easter-wings" as pattern-poem has an ease and beauty suggestive of Christian liberty, or the freedom of grace. Thus the opening sequence ushers the speaker and reader into membership in a church centered on Calvinist doctrine.

A similar concern for Calvinist theology marks the closing sequence of "The Church". This sequence contemplates "last things" in the poems "Death", "Dooms-day", "Judgement", "Heaven", and one of Herbert's best and most famous lyrics "Love" (III). This sequence tells a story of the individual's movement into heaven that emphasizes grace and sacred love. Throughout there is a concern not only for eschatology but also for the significance of these final events for present-day experience on earth. From this perspective, "Love" (III) circles back to the beginning of *The Temple* to "The Altar", and provides its spiritual meaning, replacing high-church liturgy with the love of the communion feast.

Like Donne's "Death be not proud", Herbert's poem undermines the power of "Death", since the crucifixion of Christ has transformed the frightening end, represented by a skeleton, into the avenue toward resurrection, when the mortal body will again become "fair and full of grace" (15). This redemption of the body puts one's fear of death to rest, as it looks forward to "Dooms-day", or the last judgment day, when the dust of mortality will be called from the grave, and formed into eyes and limbs again, and given a voice. "This member" (line 5 in "Dooms-day") refers to the limbs of the individual as well as to each member of the church uniting now as one body. It is unclear whether limbs or individuals whisper, *"Live you brother?"* Like Donne's "At the earth's imagined corners, blow/ Your trumpets", but with less noise and more lyricism, Herbert's "Dooms-day" uses the scene of the resurrection of the body to remind his readers of the importance of repentance now on earth: "Come away,/ Help our decay./ Man is out of order hurl'd,/ Parcel'd out to all the world" (25–28).

"Judgement" is a significantly different poem from those that precede it in the closing sequence because the speaker of *The Temple* reappears like a character in a narrative. No longer searching for a gift equivalent to Christ's passion, the speaker now understands the meaning of grace. "Judgement" is a confident poem, though it imagines the potentially unnerving final judgment by Christ. The speaker's wit now resides not in the inventiveness of his poetry ("Thanksgiving", 39–48), but in his replacement of "ev'ry mans peculiar book" (5) with the New Testament (13). This text certifies Christ's provision of grace for the speaker's sins. "Ev'ry mans peculiar book" is no doubt the record of individual acts that Christ will judge, but it could refer as well to *The Temple*. If so, "Judgement" replaces the speaker's anxious offering of his poetry as an imitation of Christ in "The Thanksgiving" (45–47) with a recognition that Christ's "book" (45), the New Testament, is the final word on the subject.

This does not mean, however, that Herbert is renouncing poetic wit. "Heaven" adopts for sacred purposes the tradition of the "echo" poem, conventionally used for secular love. Edward Herbert wrote three echo poems on romantic love, and one located in a church. George Herbert alludes indirectly to the Sidney-Herbert circle, not only through the use of this form popular with his family, but by referring again to the wit battle that the speaker tries to evoke in "The Thanksgiving". In that poem at the beginning of *The Temple,* the speaker recast the New Testament as Christ's "art of love" (47), as if Christ reinvented Ovid's work. The speaker then promises to "turn back on thee" this religious love by writing the "sacred parody" in *The Temple.* "Heaven" replaces this self-interested literary contest with a full recognition of the power of the Scriptures. "Echo", a figure from Ovid's *Metamorphosis*, is revealed to have a spiritual basis:

> Thou Echo, thou art mortall, all men know.
>   *Echo.*   No. (3–4)

An "echo" poem requires verbal ingenuity because the echo repeats but also answers and revises the previous line. The wit necessary to the poetic form is associated here with the Scriptures ("holy leaves", 11) in their ability to reflect heaven and bring a spiritual dimension to life on earth. "Heaven", like "Easter-wings", suggests that the artifice of poetry is a perfectly legitimate way to echo "those delights on high" (1).

"Love" (III) brings together Herbert's concerns about love poetry and the church. Barbara Lewalski argues that "The Church" is modeled to some extent on "The Song of Songs", the Biblical chapter traditionally interpreted as representing the love relationship between Christ and the individual.[32] In *The Temple,* "Love" (I) and (II) meditate on the issue of sacred love poetry; "Love" (III) dramatizes the love between God and man. This love is offered as the essence of the communion service. The speaker appears as a guest attending a feast; God appears as the host:

> Love bade me welcome: yet my soul drew back,
>   Guiltie of dust and sinne.
> But quick-ey'd Love, observing me grow slack
>   From my first entrance in,
> Drew nearer to me, sweetly questioning,
>   If I lack'd any thing.
>
> A guest, I answer'd, worthy to be here:
>   Love said, You shall be he.
> I the unkinde, ungratefull? Ah my deare,

> I cannot look on thee.
> Love took my hand, and smiling did reply,
> Who made the eyes but I?
>
> Truth Lord, but I have marr'd them; let my shame
> Go where it doth deserve.
> And know you not, sayes Love, who bore the blame?
> My deare, then I will serve.
> You must sit down, sayes Love, and taste my meat:
> So I did sit and eat.

In the communion service, the word host is used to describe the bread of the Eucharist. "Love" (III) represents an encounter that seems to take place both at the individual's entrance into heaven as well as during the impartation of grace to the soul during the sacrament service.

Herbert addresses several complex issues of liturgy and theology in the poem. Since the reformation, the Church of England had used a communion table to represent the last supper of the Disciples, but had required that communicants kneel when receiving communion. Conforming and dissenting Puritans called for sitting. The Arminians after 1617 were using altars or enclosing the communion table within rails and placing it altar-wise at the east end of the church in order to insist on respect for the clergy and the church. When Herbert eventually served as a minister, he called it a communion table rather than an altar (246), but required kneeling. He explains why:

> The Feast indeed requires sitting, because it is a Feast; but man's unpreparednesse asks kneeling. Hee that comes to the Sacrament, hath the confidence of a Guest, and hee that kneels, confesseth himself an unworthy one, and therefore differs from other Feasters: but hee that sits, or lies, puts up to an Apostle: Contentiousnesse in a feast of Charity is more scandal then any posture. (259)

Herbert avoids contentiousness in "Love" (III), but he expressly confirms communion as a "feast of Charity". In the poem, his speaker as guest both "confesseth himself ... unworthy" and is asked to sit, and so is given the position of an Apostle. The humility of the speaker is not false, but rather a recognition that the fall has made him "guiltie of dust and sinne" (2). The love of the host is Christ's grace in action, providing the worthiness (7), ability (12), and redemption (15) that the speaker requires. In the poem, the spiritual truth of the communion service as well as the entrance of the individual into heaven take shape according to a Calvinist model.

V. "The Church-militant"

The "Church-militant" is difficult to reconcile with other works by Herbert, including "The British Church", *Musae Responsoriae,* and his orations in 1623. In these works, often intended for king or prince, the English church and state are represented as the finest accomplishment of Christianity. In the "Church-militant", however, the true church visits England only temporarily, and, overcome by sin, escapes to America. The poem prophesies that the influence of Catholic Rome and France will bring "height of malice, and prodigious lusts,/ Impudent sinning, witchcrafts, and distrusts" (237–8), extinguishing any light remaining in the Anglican church. The poem voices a strain of Calvinist apocalyptic thought that identified the Papacy as the "Antichrist" and prophesied that the end of the world was near.[33] In this black satire of political and religious institutions, the only spark of hope comes from a theme surprisingly common to most of Herbert's works: the power of empire to spread the true faith throughout the world.

In accounts of Christian history, the "Church militant" refers to the community of believers still on earth and therefore still warring against the powers of evil, whereas the "Church triumphant" refers to those who have overcome the world and entered into glory. Herbert's poem represents Christian history as a movement of the true church from east to west, from Jerusalem to, eventually, America. This true church is continually dogged by the power of sin which forces the church out or takes over its previous manifestations. The church and sin eventually meet in apocalyptic showdown again in the east, with an uncertain ending, before God's final judgment.

The strangeness of this argument and the obscurity of the poetry have led several critics to dismiss it as "early", and therefore uncharacteristic of the mature Herbert. Hutchinson argues that the pro-Spanish and anti-French views suggest a date during the negotiations for the Spanish marriage and before King Charles married the French princess, Henrietta Maria: around 1624. Charles agrees, and places it tentatively even earlier, around 1613, after Donne's *Second Anniversary* (1612) and before 1619, since Edward Herbert's appointment as ambassador to Paris would have made impolitic the poem's unflattering comments about the French. Recent critics have questioned this approach. They argue that the pessimism in the poem reflects Herbert's view about the Church of England throughout a good portion of his life, and up to his death. Christopher Hodgkins claims that the poem represents the disappointment Herbert felt that the Church of England, particularly given the influence of the Arminians, did not fulfill the promise of the Elizabethan Settlement, with its coordination of high-church liturgy and Calvinist theology. Jeffrey Powers-Beck dates the poem between 1619–1622, and argues that it represents, first, the renewed hopes in the Virginia Company between these dates, and, later, Herbert's disillusionment with the Stuart court's lack of support for the enterprise. Both suggest that the decision to publish "The Church-militant" with the rest of *The Temple* in 1633 was a form of quiet protest against the church and state government of Charles I.[34]

It is fascinating to consider the possibility that, as Herbert wrote *Musae Responsoriae* and gave his orations, he was formulating his less positive views in "The Church-militant".[35] Hovey claims that the poem is quite similar to "The Queen of Bohemia": "Both poems are not just anti-Catholic satires, but historical-prophetic poems, portraying afflicted good in international conflict with largely Catholic inspired evil and foreseeing the triumph of good and the eventual condemnation of evil."[36] Although most of what Hovey says is accurate, "triumph of good" misrepresents "The Church-militant". Whereas "To the Queen of Bohemia" prophesies that "The sunn shall never rise/ But it shall spy some of thy victories" (45–46), and that the Queen's glory "wheeling on, it compasse shall/ This, our great sublunary ball …" ("To the same", 11–12), "The Church-militant" spans the globe and links Europe to the West Indies not through Protestant victories but through an empire, established by Spain, which clears the way for the apocalyptic movement of the true church and the power of sin.

Nevertheless, the conquest of America and the West Indies by Protestantism is imagined in all Herbert's works as not only divinely ordained but inevitable.

The poem begins with a sardonic comparison between the power of God and the piety of states:

> Much more do Common-weals acknowledge thee,
> And wrap their policies in thy decree,
> Complying with thy counsels, doing nought
> Which doth not meet with an eternall thought. (5–8)

Through irony, Herbert offers God's church as a solution to the problem of corruption and degeneration. Although human states and churches may be polluted, the true church continues on earth as the spouse of God, pure and sweet. Interestingly it is linked with the East Indies: "Spices come from the East; so did thy Spouse" (13). The poem maps out the path of the true church along the lines of the empire of the king of Spain, "tying, as with a knot, both *Indias* to his *Spaine*" (442). Thus begins the poem's effort to move from East to West Indies, and, perhaps, replace profit-seeking adventuring with a global religion. The result is the same: Protestant Christianity should cover the world.

The true church originates with the patriarchs of Judaism and Solomon's temple in Jerusalem, but moves west toward the Gentiles through Christ's crucifixion (23–5). Egyptian Christianity, established by Anthony and Macarius in the fourth century, evokes from Herbert the bigotry characteristic of European attitudes toward the conversion of foreign peoples: "Such power hath mightie Baptisme to produce/ For things misshapen, things of highest use" (45–6). Whereas editors do their best to ensure that the line is read in a way comfortable to modern readers – Egypt brings forth Christians instead of the plague of frogs during the time of Moses – there can be little doubt that the word "misshapen" refers to unconverted Egyptians as well. The mere fact that Egyptians can become Christians, meant to be remarkable, brings forth the refrain of the poem from the Psalms, celebrating God's merciful provision in the face of monstrosity: "*How deare to me, O God, thy counsels are!/ Who may to thee compare?*" Herbert is better when he returns to the European nations: he satirizes the sophistical philosophy of Greece and the warrior's glory-ethic in Rome. Here is some evidence for Herbert's pacifism, since the converted warrior's humility "taketh from the dust/ A sad repentance, not the spoils of lust" (67–8). Nevertheless, this pacifism includes empire, as imperial Rome is Christianized and reappears in Constantine's Byzantium (73–4). As in the poem "To the Queen of Bohemia," it is difficult to understand how Herbert believes a Christian empire can establish itself without bloodshed. Nevertheless there is no Christianity without empire:

> ... as before Empire and Arts made way,
> (For no lesse Harbingers would serve then they)
> So they might still, and point us out the place
> Where first the Church should raise her down-cast face.
> Strength levels grounds, Art makes a garden there;
> Then showres Religion, and makes all to bear. (83–8)

It sounds as if Herbert advocates taking over previously established empires, through events like the success of Christianity in classical Rome, Constantine's conversion, or the miraculous future transformation of the Spanish colonial empire into a Protestant realm. Surely he obscures the violence of the process through his image of the garden (87–8).[37]

The poem then circles back to the beginnings of Christian history to trace out the movement of Sin. It begins in Babylon in the east, where the Israelites were exiled, and ends with Babylon in the west, the Papacy, masquerading as the true church. Along the way, Egypt's Christianity is overpowered by false gods, Greece's by false prophets, Roman Christianity is destroyed by corrupt emperors, and finally all except Rome and the west succumb to Islam. Rome instead falls to Sin in the form of the Papacy, which includes all the religious problems of the others. As he did in *Lucus*, Herbert proclaims that the Papacy is the Antichrist, and here he adds an image of the Pope as a learned but debauched sinner (164–204). The ability of empire to pave the way for true religion is destroyed by the witchcraft of Papism, which seduces princes to bow to its power (191–204).

The last section of the poem (211–279) considers the age of the reformation. A form of degeneration in itself, since it cannot match

the purity of original Christianity (226–7), the reformation nevertheless reaches toward the future in its readiness to move to
America: "Religion stands on tip-toe in our land,/ Readie to passe to
the *American* strand" (235–6; see to 258). The Cambridge licensers
were convinced to include these lines in the publication of *The
Temple* in 1633 only through the intervention of Nicholas Ferrar,[38]
but the following lines seem even more incendiary:

> When *Sein* shall swallow *Tiber*, and the *Thames*
> By letting in them both pollutes her streams:
> When *Italie* of us shall have her will,
> And all her calender of sinnes fulfill;
> Whereby one may foretell, what sinnes next yeare
> Shall both in *France* and *England* domineer:
> Then shall Religion to *America* flee ... (241–247).

Here Herbert sounds like William Prynne in his pamphlets, complaining about the Queen Henrietta Maria on stage, or Edward Coke
in parliament, paranoid about popish conspiracies. Herbert may
refer as well to the Laudian, Arminian reforms in liturgy and theology, which, by 1633, were emphasizing high-church ceremony and
salvation by merit. Surprisingly, Catholic Spain is not a source of
pollution in England or America:

> And where of old the Empire and the Arts
> Usher'd the Gospel ever in mens hearts,
> *Spain* hath done one; when Arts perform the other,
> The Church shall come; & Sinne the Church shall smother ...
> $\qquad$ (263–266)

Here is the origin for Hutchinson's belief that this is an early poem:
given Herbert's agenda, why would he praise Catholic Spain, unless
the poem was written in part to please King James, seeking a
Spanish marriage nearly to the end of 1624? But I think we need to
consider another possibility: Herbert up to his death may have
imagined that God would use the Spanish colonial empire as a
garden for the gospel of Protestantism, just as God used the Roman
empire to establish Christianity.

V. The structure of *The Temple*

Various explanations have been offered to solve this difficult problem. However, it should be remembered that the title itself *The Temple* may not have been Herbert's, since there is no manuscript authority for the name, and Nicholas Ferrar seems to have added the title and the epigraph in his own hand.[39] It has been argued that "The Church-militant" should be considered as a separate poem, and that attention should be focused on the movement of the soul from ethical precepts to religious sanctification in "The Church-porch" and "The Church".[40] John David Walker argued that the parts of *The Temple* correspond to the parts of the Temple in Jerusalem, and the meanings ascribed to them through Christian typological interpretation.[41] But several critics have objected to his claim that "The Church-militant" corresponds to the inner most room in the Temple, the "Holy of Holies", and have rightly pointed out that Herbert's third part brings us not into a spiritual sanctuary but back to a difficult, unresolved earthly situation.[42] Stanley Fish proposed that Herbert develops his work according to a catechistical context: "the central action of the sequence is the growth of the reader-pupil into a living temple, but the living temple into which he grows already stands; it receives no addition from him, but incorporates him into membership". Fish reads "The Church-militant" as corresponding to the tradition of the *narratio*, or history of salvation, included in early catechisms.[43] Gene Edward Veith, Jr. analyzes "The Church-porch" as referring to the law, and "The Church" to the gospel, including personal communion with Christ through the Calvinist doctrine of justification by faith. He also sees the "The Church" as referring to the invisible church, and "The Church-porch" and "The Church-militant" as representative of the external, visible church operating in the world. For Veith, (229), *The Temple* creates a spatial structure of identity in which the temple within the individual is linked to an engagement with the world, either through the particular calling described in "The Church-porch" or as a participant in the larger movement of Christian history outlined in "The Church-militant".[44] Certainly critics need to become more skeptical about their desire to sever the beautiful lyrics in "The Church" from the strange vision of "The Church-militant", in which empire and the true church depend on one another.

4

1627 and Herbert's Mother

The funeral of Lady Magdalene Herbert was held on June 8, 1627, and, during the next month, George wrote 15 epigrams in Latin and 4 in Greek. Entitled *Memoriae Matris Sacrum*, the work was published on July 7 with Donne's commemorative sermon. Many have approached these poems as representing Herbert's retirement from public life. However the sequence provides evidence of the hard work he invested in preparation for office and his frustration at lack of preferment. It is true that there is very little sign of his public activity during the six years between his readiness to be a deacon in November 1624 and his ordination as priest in September 1630. We have almost no verifiable evidence of his actions in 1625 and 1628, and 1627 is marked primarily by the poems written for his mother. However, he was engaged in a number of public labors in 1626, both secular and religious. It is therefore difficult to believe that Herbert had instituted for himself a full-fledged policy of retreat from the world. The best explanation for the inactivity of 1625, 1627, and 1628 is a combination of sickness and unemployment.[1]

Herbert's unemployment is extremely surprising, given his previous positions and contacts. [2] The theory of retirement is attractive for this reason. However, recent historical studies of factions in the court and Arminianism in the church provide an alternate explanation. I have argued elsewhere that Herbert suffered from the factional antagonism between his relative and patron William Herbert, Earl of Pembroke, and the Duke of Buckingham, who during the years 1625–1628 had a near monopoly on royal patronage, both civil and ecclesiastical.[3] In addition, historians have demonstrated that, although James considered conforming Calvinists perfectly acceptable as clergy throughout most of his reign, the Arminian bishop William Laud began in 1624 to redefine Calvinism as a form of "puritanism" potentially subversive to the Crown. King Charles and the Duke of Buckingham became increasingly explicit in their support for Arminianism and their alliance with the anti-Calvinists. In 1629, the House of Commons complained that only Arminian clergy were receiving promotion within the church.[4] George Herbert's career, so promising at the outset, was probably undermined by the antagonism between Buckingham and Pembroke and the new Arminian orthodoxy developing within the Church of England.

Memoriae Matris Sacrum expresses Herbert's frustration with this situation, as well as his profound grief over the death of his mother. These two issues may be related, since the poetic sequence reveals Lady Magdalene's continuing dedication to the literary and professional success of her son. In the analysis that follows, I hope to show that recent psychoanalytic studies of the poems have unearthed the powerful and complex feelings in Herbert's attitude toward his mother. However the work also needs to be read in the context of Herbert's problematic career.

I. The events of 1625–1627

Herbert is peculiarly silent in 1625, especially given his activities in the year before, including his attendance at Parliament in February through June, and the dispensation he received to be quickly ordained as deacon in November. The only trustworthy reference to his whereabouts in 1625 is Donne's letter to Goodyer about December 21 noting that Herbert is with Donne in the Chelsea household of Magdalene and John Danvers.[5] Walton claims that Herbert reacted to the death of the Marquis of Hamilton on March 2 and King James on March 27 by retreating to live with a "Friend in *Kent*", where in "Retirement" and "solitariness" he exchanged his "Court-hopes" for "a study of Divinity".[6] In support of Walton's view, it must be admitted that Herbert did not give the Cambridge oration on May 7, 1625, honoring the death of King James, nor did he write poems for the volumes on the king or the marriage of Charles. However we also know that Herbert had already chosen to be ordained several months before James' death.

The contrast between 1625 and the next year suggests that Herbert's lack of participation in Cambridge events was the result of sickness rather than retirement or disillusionment. 1626 includes several activities reminiscent of his Cambridge years. Not only did he give an official oration as Public Orator of Cambridge before Buckingham at his installation as Chancellor of Cambridge in York House in London on July 13, Herbert also contributed to and may have helped arrange the poetic collection honoring Bacon, who died on April 9. He probably traveled to Leighton Bromswold sometime after July 13 to accept the position as canon of Lincoln Cathedral and prebend of Leighton Ecclesia granted him by Bishop John Williams. These activities hardly seem those of a recluse.[7]

Nevertheless, Herbert must have felt some alarm about his opportunities for advancement. By 1626, it was clear that Buckingham and Pembroke were enemies, and most believed that Buckingham had deprived John Williams of his position as Lord Keeper in 1625 in punishment for Williams' alliance with Pembroke. Buckingham also suspected, probably rightly, that Pembroke had led the opposition against him in the parliaments of 1625 and 1626. Pembroke's interest in influencing parliament is evident in the election of George's brother Henry in 1626 to the seat that George held in 1624. It is significant that, as far as we know, Herbert took up his duties as Public Orator for Cambridge during this period only in the month of July 1626 when an alliance between Pembroke and Buckingham was being forged through the arrangement of a marriage between Pembroke's heir, Philip Herbert's son, and Buckingham's daughter.[8]

Hopes that Herbert may have entertained about potential support from the duke would also have been moderated by the allegiance for Arminianism that Buckingham had displayed in February 1626 during the York House conference on religion. Although Herbert had several contacts and friends who were Arminians, including Bishop Lancelot Andrewes, John Richardson, Master of Trinity, and, to a small extent, Bishop Richard Neile, the program of the anti-Calvinists had consolidated considerably since March 1623, when Herbert seems to have been in their good graces. At the end of 1623,

Bishops Andrewes, Neile, and Laud had met with Prince Charles' chaplain Matthew Wren to discuss the prince's receptivity to Arminianism. In December 1624, Bishop Laud drew up for Buckingham a tract that defined Calvinism as Puritanism. After James' death, Laud developed a list for King Charles distinguishing between the "orthodox", or Arminian clergy, and the "puritan", which included all Calvinists. The argument that made the Arminians particularly successful with Charles and Buckingham was that the theology of grace and predestination led the "elect" to assume that their obedience to authority was of no importance to their salvation. The king and the Arminians united in their efforts to increase reverence for authority through a new emphasis on merit, the "beauty of holiness" in church ritual, and the saving grace of the sacraments. In June 1626, the month before Herbert gave his oration at the installation of the duke as chancellor of Cambridge, the king had banned Calvinism from press and pulpit, and refused to allow a Calvinist sermon at the Cambridge commencement exercises. After Buckingham became Chancellor, Calvinism at Cambridge was silenced.[9] Herbert's oration has been lost; one imagines that all of Herbert's powers of courtiership would have been required to avoid offending the duke on either political or religious matters. Herbert perhaps sought to make up for his oration of October 1623, when he made absolutely no reference to the duke whatsoever, but explicitly opposed his war policy. In 1626, it would have been difficult for Herbert to pass himself off as an Arminian in the oration, given his support for the Calvinist Melville's theology in *Musae Responsoriae,* as well as the tradition of Calvinist activism associated with his extended family. Certainly no patronage was forthcoming from the crown. It is remarkable how frequently the patronage received by Herbert after 1623 came from the Calvinist enemies of Buckingham: Archbishop Abbot (the dispensation to be ordained deacon immediately), Bishop Williams (ordination as deacon, the sinecure in Montgomeryshire, the prebendary at Leighton, the canonry at Lincoln), and Pembroke (seat in parliament, position at Bemerton).[10]

1627 is also instructive about Herbert's reception of patronage. One week after the publication of Herbert's verses commemorating his mother, the Crown granted the manor of Ribbesford to George and Edward Herbert, and their cousin Thomas Lawley. Henry

Herbert bought the manor for L3000, and George's portion probably made it possible for him to marry in 1629.[11] But the Crown offered employment neither to George or Edward. It is clear that Charles and Buckingham felt the need to acknowledge the value of the Herbert brothers given their previous public labors and the death of their mother, but this need did not include preferment to office. Herbert officially resigned the position of Public Orator by January 28, 1628, when the Cambridge senate voted in Robert Creighton. Walton and others have claimed that Herbert had retained the position only because of the wishes of his mother. But Herbert's letter of advice to deputy orator Robert Creighton probably dated May 6, 1627, makes it relatively clear that Herbert was planning to resign before her death.[12] He may have decided that Buckingham's suppression of Calvinism at Cambridge made it difficult to continue in the position.

II. Herbert and Bacon

In 1626, as Public Orator, Herbert contributed a Latin poem to the volume published in memory of Francis Bacon, who died on April 9. Very few other Cambridge dignitaries are represented in *Memoriae Francisci Baronis de Verulamio Sacrum,* published in London rather than Cambridge, perhaps because of Bacon's conviction for bribery in a power struggle between parliament and King James in 1621. Hutchinson believed that Herbert helped to collect the contributors for the volume since ten were from Trinity College, as were both Bacon and Herbert, and seven of these were from Westminster School.[13] Herbert's poem speaks eloquently of his belief in Bacon's historical importance:

In obitum incomparabilis Francisci Vicecomitis Sancti Albani, Baronis Verulamii

> Dum longi lentíque gemis sub pondere morbi
> > Atque haeret dubio tabida vita pede,
> Quid voluit prudens Fatum, iam sentio tandem :
> > Constat, *Aprile* uno te potuisse mori :
> Vt *Flos* hinc lacrymis, illinc *Philomela* querelis,
> > Deducant *linguae* funera sola tuae.

[*On the death of the imcomparable Francis, Viscount St. Alban, Baron Verulam*
    While you groan beneath the weight of long-
    Drawn-out illness, and with a tottering foot
    Life, wasting away, hangs on, I see at last
    What discreet destiny has willed: it is
    Certain there has never been a choice: April
    Has always been the month for you to die in, that here
    Flora with her tears, and Philomela there
    With her lamentations, may conduct
    Your idiom's lonely funeral cortege.][14]

McCloskey and Murphy's choice of the word "idiom" as a translation for "lingua" obscures the power of Herbert's use of myth.
"Lingua" refers to language or mode of expression, and thus honors
Bacon's ability as speaker and writer. However the literal meaning of
the word, tongue, clarifies the references to Flora "with her tears"
and Philomela "with her lamentations". Philomela was raped by her
sister's husband, who cut off her tongue to keep her silent. After her
own revenge, the gods turned her into a nightingale. The goddess
Flora was originally the nymph Chloris before she was raped by the
wind-god Zephyr. In Ovid's *Fasti*, as Flora tells of her rape, she
breathes out spring roses from her mouth, represented in Botticelli's
painting *Primavera*.[15] This truth of the violence behind the beauty of
spring represents the loss of the future works of Bacon because of his
death, but perhaps refers as well to the injustice done to him
through his fall from power. If so, then Bacon's written works, like
Flora's breathed-out flowers and Philomela's song, establish him as
eternal, but also do not entirely compensate for the loss of Bacon's
voice in public affairs in the preceding years.[16]

Herbert's relationship with Bacon gave the poet a good under-
standing of Bacon's philosophy, as well as an awareness that
death came before he could complete many of his works. In 1620,
Public Orator Herbert began writing official letters to Lord
Chancellor Bacon, and, during the six-month period between
November 4, 1620, to May 1, 1621, when Bacon was disgraced,
Herbert wrote 2 Latin letters and 3 Latin poems, most related to
Bacon's gift of his *Instauratio Magna* to Cambridge on October 31,
1620 (435–6, 463,467). Herbert's two letters and the first two

poems could easily have been required by University duty, but the last, much longer, and most famous of the Latin poems may have been written on his own initiative between January 27 and May 1, 1621, and was widely circulated (436, 597). Even the most dedicated of Herbert's admirers would have to admit that this outpouring of attention from Herbert suggests his interest in future patronage from the prestigious Bacon. The poem "Aethiopissa ambit Cestum Diversi Coloris Virum" ["A negro maid woos Cestus, a man of a different color"] provides evidence of an exchange between Bacon and Herbert, in which Bacon sent a diamond and Herbert the poem (437). The English poem (209) that accompanied the Latin verses comments on the relationship between Lord Chancellor and Public Orator:

> Gifts speake their Givers. For as those Refractions,
> Shining and sharp, point out your rare Perfections;
> So by the Other, you may read in mee
> (Whom Schollers Habitt and Obscurity
> Hath ere soild with Black) the colour of my state,
> Till your bright gift my darknesse did abate. (3–8)

Like Herbert's poems to King James, this verse flatters Bacon by emphasizing the wide distance between client and patron.[17]

Despite Herbert's interest in patronage from Bacon, it is also clear that, after Bacon's disgrace, Herbert was a loyal friend. At Bacon's request, Herbert translated Bacon's *Advancement of Learning* into Latin, to be published as the first book of *De Augmentis Scientia* in 1623. Bacon dedicated his *Translation of Certaine Psalmes into English Verse* to "his very good frend Mr. George Herbert" in 1625. Both Herbert's translation and Bacon's dedication may have been Bacon's method of providing whatever patronage he could for Herbert. According to Aubrey, Bacon was a frequent visitor to the Chelsea estate of Herbert's mother and stepfather. Herbert's "Church-porch" shows the direct influence of Bacon's essays "Of Discourse" and "Of Anger".[18]

Herbert's responses to *Instauratio Magna* and his translation of *The Advancement of Learning* demonstrate that he was quite familiar with some aspects of Bacon's philosophy. Herbert probably admired Bacon's belief that aphorisms as "representing a

knowledge broken, do invite men to inquire further."[19] It is fascinating to imagine Herbert, fully trained as a rhetorician, considering Bacon's theory of language developed in *The Advancement of
Learning*:

> ... men began to hunt more after words than matter, and more
> after the choiceness of the phrase, and the round and clean
> composition of the sentence, and the sweet falling of the clauses,
> and the varying and illustration of their works with tropes and
> figures than after the weight of matter, worth of subject, sound-
> ness of argument, life of invention, or depth of judgment ... Here
> therefore is the first distemper of learning, when men study
> words and not matter, ... It seems to me that Pygmalion's frenzy
> is a good emblem or portraiture of this vanity, for words are but
> the images of matter, and except they have life of reason and
> invention, to fall in love with them is all one as to fall in love
> with a picture.[20]

Herbert's use of the plain style in *The Temple* suggests some sympa-
thy for this view.

Herbert also acquired some knowledge of Bacon's scientific theories. His first poems to Bacon suggest that he had read what
Bacon had finished of *Instauratio Magna*, including the *Novum
Organon*, sent to Cambridge by the author. *The Great Instauration*
included a plan for the "total reconstruction of the sciences, arts,
and all human knowledge" according to Bacon's inductive
method of study, offered in opposition to Aristotelian logic. The
work remained unfinished at Bacon's death. Herbert's famous
longer poem to Bacon on the publication of *Instauratio Magna*
represents some of his basic theories in short poetic phrases:
"Inductionis Dominus, & Verulamij" [" lord of the inductive
method and of Verulam"] sums up Bacon's social achievement as
well as his emphasis on mastering the observation of nature first
before developing theories about it.[21] "Rerum magister unicus, at
non Artium" ["unique/ Master of factual material,/ But not of
arts"] refers to Bacon's sentence at the beginning of *Instauratio
Magna*, "Having thus coasted past the ancient arts, the next point
is to equip the intellect for passing beyond."[22] Bacon's work was
published with a frontispiece showing a ship about to sail

through the Pillars of Hercules, which, according to Bacon, represented the limits put on knowledge by the ancients and particularly Aristotle. [see Figure 1 in Chapter 2] Herbert refers to Bacon's
scientific heroism, "Alcide succumbente Stagiritico" ["champion
over/ The herculean Stagirite], at once praising Aristotle (born in
Stagira) in his abilities and taking up Bacon's metaphor for dis-
covering new territory. "Fugator Idolûm, atque nubium" [he who
puts to flight idols, and clouds] displays Herbert's knowledge of
the passage on the "Idols of the human mind" in *Novum Organon*.
Herbert's official letter of thanks for the gift of *Instauratio Magna*
uses Bacon's metaphor for the new science as the discovery of a
"new world":

[The book] is the first to point out new regions of sciences and
lands unknown to the ancients, from which thou hast gained a
more illustrious name than the discoverers of a new world have
acquired. They have discovered land, the most gross element;
thou, boundless subtleties of arts. They have discovered all things
barbarous; thou, nothing but the most refined; – elegancies
themselves thou dost display. They have relied on the magnetic
needle; thou, on the more penetrating sharpness of the intellect,
the force of which, if it had not been incredible, never, amid
such businesses as thou hast been properly distracted with,
wouldst thou have brought to light those things which have
escaped so many philosophers reveling in retirement and
leisure.[23]

It seems quite likely that Herbert and Bacon were fascinated with
each other's verbal and mental abilities. Of course, they also
reinforced their mutual belief in the God-given mission of
Western "discoveries". Herbert probably didn't agree with Bacon's
clear division between those issues properly studied through
theology and those through natural philosophy.[24] Bacon may
have appreciated Herbert as an authority on theology as did
another philosopher of the time, Edward Herbert, who dedicated
the manuscript of *De Veritate* to his brother and his secretary in
1622, asking them to excise anything contrary to religion and
good morals. Bacon seems to have appreciated Herbert's knowledge of divinity, as well, perhaps, as his religious lyrics. Bacon's

dedication of his *Translation of Certaine Psalmes into English Verse* to Herbert in 1625 suggests as much,

> The paines, that it pleased you to take, about some of my Writings, I cannot forget: which did put mee in minde, to dedicate to you, this poore Exercise of my sicknesse. Besides, it being my manner for Dedications, to choose those that I hold most fit for the Argument, I thought, that in respect of Divinitie, and Poesie, met (whereof the one is the Matter, the other the Stile of this little Writing) I could not make better choice. So, with significance of my Love and Acknowledgment, I ever rest
>
> Your affectionate Frend, Fr: St. Alban.[25]

Herbert may have identified with Bacon's illness and his exclusion from public office. Herbert uses the same word about Bacon in his commemorative poem in 1626 and about himself in 1627 in Epigram #7 in the verses about his mother: "tabidus", wasting away.

III. Memoriae Matris Sacrum

Several critics have found evidence in these poems for Herbert's retreat from the world. F.E. Hutchinson reads the sequence for information about the biography:

> His movements in the next two years [1627–8] are difficult to trace. From the seventh poem in memory of his mother, written in the summer of 1627, he appears to be living in a country cottage (*domuncula*) with a luxuriant flower-garden. He has chosen a humble lot (*parvam piamque semitam*), but still finds difficulty in reconciling himself to it. (xxxiii)

W. Hilton Kelliher disagrees with this interpretation because it minimizes the value that Herbert found in retirement: "Hutchinson's reading ... is the exact opposite of Herbert's cry against the fate that will not leave him in peaceful obscurity but visits him with new afflictions."[26] E. Pearlman's psychoanalytic reading illuminates "the crucial role of the maternal bond" for Herbert, but Pearlman finds that the poems create fantasies of reunification with the mother in order to ward off "political, economic, and social reality": "Not just particular images or entire poems but Herbert's life work as a whole therefore consists of the creation of an imaginary structure designed to bulwark him against the terrors of an outside world."[27]

Herbert's commemorative verses for his mother do praise the retired life and suggest quite strongly that the poet would like to disappear into "peaceful obscurity", or even follow his mother into the next world. However the work makes it clear that this desire for isolation is problematic, and the sequence moves the poet toward accepting his position in a larger world, including its demand for social engagement and productive labor.

The first poem introduces several issues central to the sequence, including the imagery of tears and water, as well as the poet's extraordinary claim to be his mother's only child. I use the translation of Deborah Rubin:

> Ah Mater, quo te deplorem fonte? Dolores
> 　　　Quae guttae poterunt enumerare meos ?
> Sicca meis lacrymis Thamesis vicina videtur,
> 　　　Virtutúmque choro siccior ipse tuo.
> In flumen moerore nigrum si funderer ardens,
> 　　　Laudibus haud fierem sepia iusta tuis.
> Tantùm istaec scribo gratus , ne tu mihi tantùm
> 　　　Mater: & ista Dolor nunc tibi Metra parit.[28]

> [Ah Mother, where's the fountain to lament you?
> 　　　What drops can measure up my grief?
> Neighboring Thames seems dry, to all my tears;
> 　　　I, dryer than your virtues' chorus.
> If, burning, I were poured in the dark river
> 　　　I'd never be fit ink for praise.
> Grateful, I write this, lest to me alone
> 　　　You're "Mater"; grief gives birth to meter.][29]

Curiously, the poet seems to deny his siblings (of which there were nine, seven living) by claiming that he alone entertains his mother's memory unless he can communicate her value in public verse: "lest to me alone/ You're 'Mater.'" The pun on "Mater" and "Metra" in the last line implies that he will turn his mother into verse by giving birth to a poetic image of her. Since "metra" means measure, the

flood of grief and tears felt by the poet will be measured out and
controlled through the meters of poetry.

This claim to possess the mother recurs in the seventh poem of
the sequence. Here the poet cries out in protest against being
haunted by a terrible shade of his mother rather than the human
being so important to him. He asks instead for a private world that
the two can share. I quote the poem in full because it bears directly
on the issue of retirement:

> Pallida materni Genij atque exanguis imago,
> In nebulas similésque tui res gaudia nunquid
> Mutata? & pro matre mihi phantasma dolosum
> Uberáque aerea hiscentem fallentia natum?
> Vae nubi pluuiâ graudae, non lacte, meásque
> Ridenti lacrymas quibus unis concolor vnda est.
> Quin fugias?   mea non fuerat tam nubila Iuno,
> Tam segnis facies aurorae nescia vernae,
> Tam languens genitrix cineri supposta fugaci:
> Verùm augusta parens, sanctum os caelóque locandum,
> Quale paludosos iamiam lictura recessus
> Praetulit Astraea, aut solio Themis alma vetusto
> Pensilis, atque acri dirimens Examine lites.
> Hunc vultum ostendas, & tecum, nobile spectrum,
> Quod superest vitae, insuman : Solísque iugales
> Ipse tuae solùm adnectam, sine murmure, thensae,
> Nec querar ingratos, studijs dum tabidus insto,
> Effluxisse dies, suffocatámue Mineruam,
> Aut spes productas, barbatáque somnia vertam
> In vicium mundo sterili, cui cedo cometas
> Ipse suos tanquam digno pallentiáque astra.
>   Est mihi bis quinis laqueata domuncula tignis
> Rure; brevísque hortus, cuius cum vellere florum
> Luctatur spacium, qualem tamen eligit aequi
> Iudicij dominus, flores vt iunctiùs halent
> Stipati, rudibúsque volis imperuius hortus
> Sit quasi fasciculus crescens, & nidus odorum.
> Hìc ego túque erimus, variae suffitibus herbae
> Quotidie pasti: tantùm verum indue vultum
> Affectûsque mei similem; nec languida misce

Ora meae memori menti: ne dispare cultu
Pugnaces, teneros florum turbemus odores,
Atque inter reliquos horti crescentia fœtus
Nostra etiam paribus marcescant gaudia fatis.

[Pale bloodless shade of my mother's spirit, have my joys been changed to mists and things like you? Do you, cunning apparition, take my mother's place, breasts of air deceiving your gaping-mouthed child? Woe, cloud, heavy with rain not milk, mocking my tears, the color of water, why don't you go away? My Juno wasn't so gloomy, so slow a form, ignorant of vernal dawn, so languid a mother, substituted for fleeting ashes. Truly, she was a majestic parent; a sacred face worthy to be placed in the sky, like that Astraea bore when she was ready to forsake her marshy retreats, or that of kind Themis, raised aloft on her ancient throne, ending strife with keen judgement. Show that countenance, and with you noble specter, I'll expend what remains of life. I myself will hitch the horses of the Sun to your chariot without a murmur. Nor will I bewail the thankless days that have passed by as I, wasting away, pursued my studies – Minerva strangled – or hopes postponed, and my maturer dreams I'll cast off into the barren world of mutability, to which, for it deserves them, I leave its comets and pale stars.

I have a little paneled house in the country with twice five beams and a small garden where downy flowers contend for space. But a discerning owner would choose just such a place so that the compacted flowers might breathe in accord, and so that, impassable to uncouth feet, the garden might be like a blooming nosegay and a nest of odors. Here, you and I shall daily feast on the incense of many herbs. Only assume your true expression, similar in feeling to mine, and don't confuse this faint face with the one I remember, lest we, at odds because of different situations, confound the tender odors of the flowers, and lest, among the other fruits of the garden, our growing joys [the flowers] begin to droop because of fates like ours.][30]

Pearlman and Rubin consider the "unresolved Oedipal attachment" implicit in this poem as well as in the sequence. "The facts – that George's father died when he was three years old, a crucial age in terms of the resolution of oedipal conflicts, and that Magdalene

Herbert married Sir John Danvers, a man in his twenties, when George was not quite sixteen – support this possibility."[31] Pearlman notes the remarkable mixture of the erotic and the infantile in the fantasy of intimacy in epigram #7, and Rubin comments on how the poem splits Magdalene Herbert into virtuous good mother and abandoning bad mother through the imagery of breast-feeding. Both critics notice that the pastoral imagery in the poem, creating a *locus amoenus*, heightens the sense of the exclusivity of the relationship.[32]

But more attention needs to be paid to the lines on the poet's career:

Nec querar ingratos, studijs dum tabidus insto,
Effluxisse dies, suffocatámue Mineruam,
Aut spes productas, barbatáque somnia vertam
In vicium mundo sterili, cui cedo cometas
Ipse suos tanquam digno pallentiáque astra. (17–21)

[Nor will I bewail the thankless days that have passed by as I, wasting away, pursued my studies – Minerva strangled – or hopes postponed, and my maturer dreams I'll cast off into the barren world of mutability, to which, for it deserves them, I leave its comets and pale stars.]

The poet imagines renouncing his work to join in blissful union, but the union serves as an alternative to uncompensated labor. If, as Hutchinson claims, Herbert lived in a country cottage with a luxuriant flower-garden, he spent his time in studies and hopes that should properly have been brought to fruition much earlier. The phrase "barbatáque somnia" is especially good in this regard: literally, "dreams that have grown a beard." The phrase suggests maturity, but also implies that the dreamer has grown from youth to manhood without the realization of expectations that he has held for a very long time. The result of such frustrated effort is that the poet is "tabidus" – "wasting away": he decays in his country cottage, because of "suffocatámue Mineruam" – "Minerva strangled". This does not sound like a life he would have chosen for himself, but rather a sense of thwarted potential. He has been led to believe that through his studies he would be contributing to the world in a productive way, but these efforts have been "thankless".

The image of Minerva, the goddess of wisdom and the Latin version of Pallas Athena, recalls the numerous references to Athena in Herbert's University poems. The verses in commemoration of Prince Henry, poems to Frederick, Elector Palatine, and *Musae Responsoriae* (#6,37) allude to Athena, and often Herbert does so to evoke the wisdom of Cambridge. If so, in these later Latin verses, the poet laments the waste of his acquired skills and education.

Minerva also recalls the image of his mother as goddess in the earlier lines of the poem: "Truly, she was a majestic parent; a sacred face worthy to be placed in the sky, like that Astraea bore when she was ready to forsake her marshy retreats, or that of kind Themis, raised aloft on her ancient throne, ending strife with keen judgement." Themis was the goddess of law who counseled Jupiter. Astraea, her daughter, represented the purity and innocence of justice, and was the last of the gods to leave the earth after the golden age. The death of the mother is associated with the loss of justice. Minerva has been "strangled" just as the "sacred face" of Themis has given way before the "pale bloodless shade". The private relationship sought by the poet is one in which this justice would be restored. The poet asks, "Only assume your true expression, similar in feeling to mine, and don't confuse this faint face with the one I remember ..." Psychoanalytic readings by Pearlman and Rubin argue that this poem gives voice to a powerful identification with the mother.[33] In an earlier epigram, the poet praises his mother for her verbal abilities ("Lepos seuerus, Pallas mixta Gratijs", [stern wit, Minerva mixed with the Graces]), and thanks her for teaching him how to write (#2:30).[34]

One of his mother's primary virtues, according to George, was the successful performance of her social duties. This becomes explicit in the following letter Herbert wrote to his mother in 1622:

> Your last letter gave me Earthly preferment, and kept Heavenly for your self: but, would you divide and choose too? Our College Customs allow not that, and I should account my self most happy if I might change with you; for I have always observ'd the thred of Life to be like other threds or skenes of silk, full of snarles and incumbrances: Happy is he, whose bottom is wound up and laid ready for work in the New *Jerusalem* – For my self, *dear Mother*, I always fear'd sickness more then death, because

sickness hath made me unable to perform those Offices for which I came into the world, and must yet be kept in it; but you are freed from that fear, who have already abundantly discharg'd that part, having both ordered your Family, and so brought up your Children that they have attain'd to the years of Discretion, and competent Maintenance. (372–3)

Herbert tells his mother that he would be most happy "if I might change with you", not because he would choose heavenly prefer-ment over earthly, but because he would like to be in his mother's position. In his view, she has fulfilled her duties on earth, and so is ready for heaven. He is afraid that sickness will prevent him from performing "Offices" which are earthly but divinely required. This passage demonstrates that, according to the Protestant doctrine of vocation, the duties of one's social role cannot be replaced by an exclusive attention to one's spiritual estate, but must be pursued with the two in coordination. As the passage above makes clear, for Herbert to identify with his mother is to come to fruition both professionally and spiritually.

Epigram #7 certainly imagines the abandonment of this plan and a full retreat into a private pastoral world. But the rest of the sequence moves the poet away from such a solution. Epigram #17 in Greek is clearest on this issue:

> I mourn my mother, as well as other men
> Who do not make her now my clan's
> Especial guardian, but, since she was virtuous,
> Want her for their own mother.
> It isn't very strange they claim her,
> For it isn't right or possible to keep
> Behind a single door the common blessings
> Of water or of light. She was the purest law,
> Beauty's vision to the world, the glass of God. (1–9) [35]

The poet no longer claims to be his mother's only child. He is now not only a member of a clan (2), but cognizant of the people outside the family who grieve the loss of Lady Magdalene Herbert (1). The imagery of water and light (8) used throughout the sequence now represents the bounty of Lady Magdalene bestowed on society, or the "common" wealth (7). The mother becomes "the purest law" (9), and her face is made celestial. Perhaps here the dyad of mother and child is given up for the wider context of the social law. Remembering the mother's significance "to the world" requires the poet to know himself according to his position within society. However, identification with the mother will not be given up; now she has become a mirror for all: "the glass of God".

The poetic sequence after epigram #7 is a process of expanding outward to include the family and the nation. It is true that epigram #2 considers the mother in terms of her benevolent social works, but this perspective is muted by the intense focus on mother and child in #3–7. But epigram #9 speaks of a close circle of mourners who weep together rather than attend to the events of state. Herbert lists the recent developments of the Protestant battle with the Catholics in the Thirty Years' War, but marks these events as incapable of drawing the group away from their grieving. Nevertheless his details show quite a firm grasp of current events. "The king equips a fleet" so that Buckingham can sail out on June 27 to support the Huguenot rebellion at La Rochelle, and in hopes of capturing the Isle of Rhé. Herbert even comments on the delay of the fleet's departure because of the wind (15–17).[36] "Tilly pursues the Danes", ravaging Jutland in the summer of 1627 after his Catholic forces destroyed the Protestant forces of Christian IV of Denmark at Lutter on August 26, 1626. "The French pursue the sea", because, in the same month Herbert's mother died, France and England went to war with each other.[37] "Nos flendo: haec nostrûm tessera sola ducum"; [we pursue weeping: this is the only token of our leaders]: the imagery of water links the mourning circle only in a cursory way to the naval expeditions of England.[38] Nevertheless it is significant that the experience of mourning is juxtaposed to a nation defined completely in terms of Protestant battle. The poem implies that this group needs a temporary license to grieve, not that they will never return to the outside world. Epigram #10 follows this plan by expanding out of the circle of mourners to include the entire British realm: the constant rain becomes an image for an empire in mourning: "Country, city, and court bewail you now. England, the two Gaelic realms and ancient Wales weep for you." Herbert's favorite image of England surrounded by a protecting sea is transformed into national bereavement: "Now not a nook of these islands sees fair weather, and the sea no more encompasses but rather floods them all."[39]

The crucial poem of transition in this process is epigram #8. This poem is positioned after the dream of unity with the mother and before the redirection of the poet's gaze towards a larger community. Epigram #8 acknowledges a conflict between the virtues of a retired life and one's calling:

> Paruam piámque dum lubenter semitam
>> Grandi reaéque praefero,
> Carpsit malignum sydus hanc modestiam
>> Vinúmque felle miscuit.
> Hinc fremere totus & minari gestio
>> Ipsis severus orbibus;
> Tandem prehensâ comiter lacernulâ
>> Susurrat aure quispiam,
> Haec fuerat olim potio Domini tui,
>> Gusto probóque Dolium.

[While I prefer with pleasure the small and holy pathway to the grand and guilty highway, a malignant star has destroyed this moderation, and mixed bile with my wine.[40] From this time all my being burns with rage and bluster: I lower against the very heavens. At length someone takes me by the cloak in a friendly way and whispers in my ear: "this once was your Lord's bitter draught." I taste and approve the vintage.[41]]

Kelliher finds here not only an echo of "The Collar", but also "Herbert's cry against the fate that will not leave him in peaceful obscurity but visits him with new afflictions."[42] These afflictions include the death of his mother, but also the necessity to write public verse again and, I believe, to move beyond the desire for a hidden retired life. The poem opens by evoking Jesus' urging to avoid the "wide ... gate" and "broad ... way, that leadeth to destruction", and to choose the "strait ... gate" and "narrow ... way, which leadeth unto life" (Matt. 7:13–14). Nevertheless, the poem ends with the deeper question of the New Testament, "Are ye able to drink of the cup that I shall drink of ... ?" (Matt. 20:22). The poem implies that the moral discretion of choosing the narrow way cannot compare to the willingness to suffer afflictions in public for a larger purpose. Christ's sacrifice required contact with "the grand and guilty highway".

Perhaps the poet imagines that this exposure to the public eye will only occur through the publication of the sequence, and that he himself will withdraw again into his country cottage. The last poem, epigram #19, in fact claims that he will never write again, although Kelliher suggests that Herbert may refer here only to Latin verse.[43] But the poem also implies that he gives up verse not to retreat into a pastoral idyll but to recommit himself to the studies and hopes he seriously considered renouncing in epigram #7:

> Excussos manibus calamos, falcémque resumptam
> Rure, sibi dixit Musa fuisse probro.
> Aggreditur Matrem (conductis carmine Parcis)
> Funeréque hoc cultum vindicat aegra suum.
> Non potui non ire acri stimulante flagello:
> Quin Matris superans carmina poscit honos.
> Eia, agedum scribo: vicisti, Musa: sed audi,
> Stulta: semel scribo, perpetuò vt sileam.

> [The Muse has made it known
> The laying down of quills from hands,
> The taking up again of scythes in fields,
> Have been discourtesy to her.
> She to my mother goes (the Fates
> By song bought off) and by this death
> Grown ill, claims her own
> Kind of worship there. I could not stay
> Away: her flagellation drove me.
> More, my mother's excellence, her honor,
> Must needs be sung to. Well then, I write.
> Muse, you win. But hear,
> O vain one! This one time I write
> To be forever still.][44]

This poem returns not to the pastoral but to the georgic: "Excussos manibus calamos, falcèmque resumptam/ Rure, sibi dixit Musa fuisse probro" (1–2) ["The Muse has made it known/ The laying down of quills from hands,/ The taking up again of scythes in fields,/ Have been discourtesy to her."] The Muse requires that the poetry in praise of his mother be written instead of the work of reaping. "Rure" (2) repeats epigram #7, "Est mihi bis quinis laqueata domuncula tignis/ Rure" ["I have a little paneled house in the country with twice five beams"]. But in epigram #19, this country has crops to be harvested: "The taking up again of scythes." Herbert's last poem in the sequence finds an elegant solution to the problem of his career: he represents himself somewhere in between pastoral retreat and a full return to "the grand and guilty highway", as a farmer laboring in the fields, pursuing his studies although without reward, ready for either a quiet life or preferment to office.

5
The Temple: Poems on Grace, Employment, and the Church

Herbert's ordination as a country parson in the small parish of Bemerton in 1630 is traditionally identified as the primary event of the last years of his life. However, the significance of this event remains unclear. Walton conflates 1625–1630 as those years when Herbert retires from the worldly life, resists but eventually dedicates himself to the ministry, and is rewarded by King Charles and Bishop Laud through the preferment to Bemerton. Amy Charles persuasively refutes Walton's account of the involvement of Charles and Laud in the preferment, but finds the living to be the culmination of Herbert's early desire to enter the ministry. Ronald Cooley, however, has argued that the living of Bemerton was in fact Herbert's first step toward higher promotion. Michael Schoenfeldt suggests that Herbert never gave up his interest in advancement or his keen powers of courtiership. Many of Herbert's biographers have approached his ordination and early death from an illness at the age of 40 as the final chapter of a completed life, but Herbert himself may have had very different expectations.[1]

I have argued elsewhere that Herbert understood the grant of money rather than position from the Crown in 1627 as a sign that high ecclesiastical preferment would not be forthcoming.[2] Whereas I think Cooley may be right that Herbert hoped to advance, it is also likely that Herbert thought it possible that he would live out his life in a country post, especially given the direction of ecclesiastical patronage in the court. As the Commons made clear in 1629, its last session before the beginning of Personal Rule, Charles was passing over Calvinist clergy for an Arminian orthodoxy.[3] The living at

Bemerton was open because the king had promoted Dr. Walter Curle, who held the living as a non-resident, to the bishopric of Bath and Wells, but Curle was a Laudian.[4] Just as Herbert characterizes himself as a farmer in the country at the end of the poems commemorating his mother, there is evidence in the poetry and his pastoral manual that he was preparing himself to accept a country life. This view is not the same as Walton's, because he assumes that, as soon as Herbert was ready, Charles and Laud appointed him to a church post. Also, Walton sees any sort of ordination as a renunciation of ambition.[5] I have argued that Herbert sought ordination in 1624, before the death of King James and before the Arminians consolidated their power, because he believed it was his most trustworthy route to advancement. Also, unlike Walton's view, I believe Herbert never lost interest in the future of Protestantism in the state and the world.

The two manuscripts of *The Temple* shed some light on Herbert's career.[6] The longer and later "B" manuscript includes lyrics that mark a shift from unemployment to employment in a church position that is felt to be rewarding and productive. The earlier "W" manuscript includes several poems on the unfulfilled desire for a position: "Employment" (I) and (II), "Praise" (I), and "Affliction" (I). A number of poems in "B" have similar concerns: "Submission", "The Quip", and "The Answer". But the "B" manuscript includes as well poems of fruition: "The Crosse", "Aaron", "The Banquet", "The Invitation", and "The Windows". Although there is some evidence that Herbert may have delayed his ordination as a priest because of a sense of unworthiness ("The Priesthood"), the overwhelming majority of the poems that bear on this subject suggest that the poet waited quite a significant period of time between his readiness for employment and his preferment to a position.[7]

The poems also record a very likely reason for the postponement of his preferment: the Calvinist theology of grace that pervades these lyrics would not have made Herbert attractive to an Arminian court. Several critics have shown how the dynamics of grace determine the movement of individual poems in "The Church", including "The Holdfast", "Dialogue", "Redemption", "The Pearl", and "The Posie".[8] The sequence also refers to predestination, particularly in "The Thanksgiving", and "The Water-course", a topic that had been outlawed as a subject for sermons in 1622, 1626 and 1628.[9] In

March 1630, a month before Herbert was installed at Bemerton, John Davenant, Bishop of Salisbury, gave a sermon on predestination before the court, and was reprimanded for it by King Charles before the Privy Council.[10]

Nevertheless, Herbert continued to map out in his poetry a Jacobean middle way between high ceremony and non-conformity.[11] In October 1630, a month after Herbert became a priest, Henry Sherfield, an official in town government, broke a stained-glass window in St. Edmund's church in Salisbury as a protest against Davenant's refusal to replace the window with plain glass. Davenant brought Sherfield before Star Chamber, which fined him L500.[12] Like Davenant, Herbert insisted on the value of the "sacred ritual" of the established church and the authority of the clergy, as he also resisted the new Arminian orthodoxy. His poem "The Windows" displays his sense of the value of church ornament as it also internalizes its meaning. Like "The Altar", the poem brings together ceremony with Calvinism: the power of the church resides not in a physical image, or in the reverence for "the beauty of holiness" emphasized by the Laudians, but in preaching brought to life through the minister's embodiment of the gospel.[13] We will find that Herbert's poetry on the church maintains the Jacobean ideal as it acknowledges the dangers of both Arminianism and non-conformity.

I. The events of 1628–1633

Although Herbert did not receive a position from the Crown after the publication of his Latin poems commemorating his mother, he must have acquired a substantial amount of the L3000 that his brother Henry paid for the manor of Ribbesford given by the king to George, Edward, and Thomas Lawley. It seems likely that this money gave Herbert the ability to marry. He officially resigned the position of Public Orator of Cambridge by January 28, 1628, and by March of 1629, he was married to Jane Danvers, a relative of his stepfather.[14] Walton reports that in 1628, Herbert was living with Henry Danvers, earl of Danby, brother to John Danvers, in Dauntesey, near Chippenham. Aubrey claims that Herbert lived with Danby after the marriage.[15] On March 5, 1629, Herbert married Jane Danvers, daughter to Charles Danvers of Baynton House, in Edington Church, Baynton. Herbert was connecting himself even more closely with the family of his stepfather, a family known for its Protestant activism. Henry Danvers had served as Philip Sidney's page in the Low Countries, and was probably present at the battle of Zutphen, where Sidney was fatally wounded. Henry and his brother Charles (to be distinguished from Jane's father) continued to fight in the Protestant wars in the Netherlands, and served in Ireland under Essex as Lords Lieutenants in the late 1590's. Henry's brother Charles was executed in 1601 for participation in the Essex rebellion. After Charles' execution, Henry was named heir to the estates of his father after a declaration of King James and a special act of parliament in 1603. Henry was on good terms with the Stuart court: he was created Earl of Danby in 1626, and sworn in as a member of the Privy Council on July 20, 1628.[16]

Walton pointed out the hurried nature of the marriage between George Herbert and Jane Danvers – it took place during Lent without the usual banns and license.[17] Walton claims that friends wisely arranged the marriage; however, these hurried events could also be explained in terms of Herbert's desire to be prepared for clerical duties. Herbert's *Country Parson* urges priests to marry to ensure peace and to control gossip in the parish (236–9). Herbert was also in good enough health in May 1629 to travel to Lincoln to give a sermon in the cathedral.[18] During this period, he may have also settled on Wiltshire as a home, since several members of the Danvers family lived there. John Danvers acquired an estate in Lavington, Wiltshire, on July 10, 1628, through marriage with his second wife, and soon resided there[19]. Herbert's eventual living in Bemerton, near Salisbury, is also quite close to Wilton House, the home of the Earls of Pembroke, and Herbert may have served as chaplain there. Not only the Earls of Pembroke, but Henry and John Danvers, are acknowledged as innovators in the practice of English gardening.[20] It is probable that these families located within Wiltshire provided Herbert with a social and patronage network that supported his entrance into the priesthood, and may have given him at least limited reason to hope for future preferment. In any case, a deed of presentation to Bemerton St. Andrew and Fugglestone St. Peter was made out to Herbert from Westminster on April 16, 1630. On April 26, Herbert was instituted by John Davenant, Bishop of Salisbury, at the Cathedral, and Herbert was installed at Bemerton on the same day. Herbert missed the first possible date for ordination on May 16, although his curate Nathanael Bostocke was ordained on that date. Charles argues that Herbert again gave his required sermon in Lincoln Cathedral in May. Finally, on September 19, 1630, Herbert was ordained priest in Salisbury Cathedral.[21]

There is some question about who exactly was responsible for naming Herbert to the living at Bemerton. It is clear that the king would have had the right to award the position since Charles promoted the previous rector Dr. Walter Curle to his new post as Bishop of Bath and Wells. However, the living was ordinarily within the gift of the Earl of Pembroke, and the patron's wishes would have been considered.[22] David Novarr has disputed the claim that William Herbert, third earl of Pembroke, took an active interest in George's preferment.[23] The deed of presentation was dated April 16, 1630, and, since William Herbert, the third earl, had died on April 10, Philip Herbert, the fourth earl, may have named George Herbert to the living. However, Curle was promoted on October 29, 1629, and confirmed on December 4, 1929.[24] The living was therefore open for five months when William Herbert was alive. It also seems very unlikely that the decision to offer the post to George was first made between April 10 and 16, 1630, since George was present and ready to be instituted at Salisbury Cathedral ten days after the presentation, on April 26. Philip's ability to take the time to offer the living to George and for George to accept it between April 10 and 16 is made even more improbable since, on April 12, Philip was competing with Laud in a close election to succeed his brother William as Chancellor of Oxford (Herbert was defeated by nine votes).[25] It is far more logical to assume that, after the living fell open on October 29, 1629, William offered it to George. After some thought, George agreed, and Philip oversaw the deed of presentation six days after William's death.

During the three years of his work as a minister, Herbert's activities were markedly different from his previous life. He chose to live in the rectory across the lane from Bemerton church, although both required restoration, and he seems to have spent at least L200 on the rectory.[26] The Bemerton church is extremely small in comparison to other churches in his experience, particularly those associated with Westminster school and Trinity College. Most of his parishioners were country people, and his

own words on the subject suggest some irritation with their lack
of sophistication (233). One of his letters to his brother Henry at
court simply asks for news, as if the everyday life in Bemerton was
rather mundane (379). Aubrey reports that, after his death,
Herbert "was buryed (according to his own desire) with the
singing service for the buriall of the dead, by the singing men of
Sarum", and therefore his burial in the Bemerton chancel
"without any inscription" may also have been his choice.[27] Arthur
Woodnoth testifies that Herbert's motto, "less than the least of all
of God's mercies," was meant to distinguish him from any
"worldly Honor", especially those associated with class status.[28]

   On the other hand, in 1630, he became the master of a household
that included around 10 people, including his wife, two or three
daughters of his sister Margaret, and six servants. As Charles makes
clear, the money from the Ribbesford manor, the living at
Bemerton, and Herbert's sinecures were substantial enough to
provide him with more financial independence than he had ever
had before.[29] He began a program of restoring Leighton Ecclesia,
supported by the Ferrar brothers, and his efforts at raising money at
court through his brother Henry were accompanied by his own
substantial contributions.[30] His duties in the area included not only
the services at the chapel of Bemerton, but also those at the parish
church of Fugglestone St. Peter's, a significantly larger structure just
outside Wilton House grounds. According to Aubrey, he also served
as the chaplain at Wilton House.[31] *The Country Parson* speaks
frequently of the role of a chaplain, and the need to maintain one's
religious integrity, despite the pressures of social etiquette (226,
248–9, 286). This suggests that Herbert was present at Wilton House
during events that were not exclusively religious. Rosemond Tuve
conjectures that "A Parodie", most likely an imitation of a song by
William Herbert, was composed for the entertainments at Wilton
House.[32] Although Walton's accounts of Herbert's trips to Salisbury
Cathedral may be fanciful, certainly Herbert would have spent some
time with Bishop John Davenant, who was Lady Margaret Professor
of Divinity at Cambridge until 1621, attended the Synod of Dort in
1618–19, and delivered sermons at court.[33] We have only a few
letters written by and to Herbert during this period, but many of
Herbert's papers were destroyed after his death, and, according to
Novarr, Walton was not above changing or deleting letters that did

not support his view of his subjects' lives.[34] Aside from the Ferrar brothers, Henry Herbert, Philip Herbert and his wife Lady Anne, it seems likely that Herbert was also in touch with his wife's family in Baynton; Sir John Danvers; John's brother, Henry Danvers, the Earl of Danby; Edward Herbert; Thomas Herbert; Bishop John Williams; John Donne; and perhaps Archbishop Abbott, Francis Nethersole, as well as former colleagues of Bacon. It is useful to remember that two members of the nobility close to Herbert during this period, Philip Herbert, Earl of Pembroke and Montgomery, and Henry Danvers, Earl of Danby, were members of the Privy Council.[35]

During the period of 1628–1633, the Protestant cause was still very much at stake on the continent and in the Americas. Gustavus Adolphus, King of Sweden, entered the battle with the Catholic Hapsburgs in Germany in June 1630 and was consistently successful until his death in 1632. Although Charles was committed to recovering the Palatinate for his sister and brother-in-law, the refusal to call parliament made it difficult for him to support the continental Protestants. Also, peace agreements were reached with France in 1629 and Spain in 1630, and Spain had promised to seek the restoration of the Palatinate. In June 1632, Thomas Roe and Francis Nethersole spoke for Elizabeth of Bohemia when they tried to move Charles against peace with Spain and toward an alliance with the Dutch, but, for his actions, Nethersole was dismissed from Elizabeth's service through Charles' influence. Hopes for restoration were dimmed but not destroyed when in November 1632, Elizabeth's husband Frederick, Elector Palatine, died, as did Gustavus Adolphus.[36]

During this period, English Anglicans and Puritans continued to settle North America. John Winthrop was named governor of the Massachusetts Bay Colony in 1629, and brought 1,000 settlers to Salem in 1630. The reasons he gave for colonizing New England were very similar to those in Herbert's "Church-militant": making the gospel available to the "new world", bringing the fullness of the Gentiles into the kingdom of God, and escaping God's judgment coming upon the corrupt churches of Europe ("Reasons for Emigrating to New England", 1631). In subsequent years, various kinds of settlements were planned in Maryland, the Carolinas, and Maine/ New Hampshire.[37]

Certainly Herbert would have kept abreast of these events, given his interest in the colonization of the Americas and continental

Protestantism ("To the Lady Elizabeth Queen of Bohemia", *Memoriae Matris Sacrum*, #9). It is well known that the publication of *The Temple* was delayed because of lines in "The Church-militant": "Religion stands on tip-toe in our land,/ Readie to passe to the *American* strand" (235–6).[38] Herbert critics seem ready to assume that this poem was a naïve early work, and that the lines refer to settlement in the Virginia Colony in 1609 and shortly after. However, Herbert continued to advocate engagement in colonization particularly for younger sons in *The Country Parson*, written in the 1630's (278). It is also clear that Herbert intended "The Church-militant" to be published with "The Church" in 1633. It is therefore quite possible that the famous lines in "The Church-militant" refer to Winthrop and the Massachusetts Bay Colony, as the Cambridge licenser seemed to fear. Herbert could also be alluding to the increasing power of the Arminians or the Catholic court developing around Queen Henrietta Maria in the following lines:

> When *Sein* shall swallow *Tiber*, and the *Thames*
> By letting in them both pollutes her streams:
> When *Italie* of us shall have her will
> And all her calender of sinnes fulfill;
> Whereby one may foretell, what sinnes next yeare
> Shall both in *France* and *England* domineer:
> Then shall Religion to *America* flee ... (241–247).

Herbert's later poem "The British Church" maintains the attack on Catholic *"Italie"* evident in "The Church-militant" and *Musae Responsoriae*, and *The Country Parson* continues to argue against the "Papist" (262–3). "Church-rents and schismes" calls for the conversion of "Asia and Europe ... and ev'n all Africk."

Walton's hagiography is most evident in his account of Herbert's preparation for death. This description has done more damage to an accurate assessment of Herbert's life and poetry than any biographical error. According to Walton, Herbert said on his deathbed that his English poems were "a picture of the many spiritual Conflicts that have past betwixt God and my Soul, before I could subject mine to the will of Jesus, *my Master*: in whose service I have now found perfect freedom." The quotation attributed to Herbert is without external verification and probably represents Walton's own view. However, critics repeat this phrase as if it were Herbert's direct testimony. Novarr demonstrated long ago that many of Walton's accounts are without any basis in fact. According to Novarr, Walton developed his biographies in order to substantiate his own perspective, in this case, the "gospel of the fitness of the holy life for men of worldly attainment" (326). Walton's source for this scene was Edmund Duncon, who, according to Walton and the Ferrars, received the poems from Herbert and delivered them to Nicholas. Walton describes Herbert on his deathbed giving his poems to Duncon, asking that Nicholas Ferrar oversee publication or destroy them if he found them to be without merit. We know that Nicholas did oversee the publication of *The Temple*, and Duncon was consulted directly by Walton. Nevertheless Duncon spoke from memory about an event that had occurred forty years before. Novarr demonstrates how much of the speech on the poems presented by Walton is a collection of details from Oley and Ferrar's preface to *The Temple* rather than testimony from Duncon. John Ferrar's account of the poems does corroborate Walton's claim that Herbert asked Nicholas to decide whether or not the poems should be published, but he mentions nothing remotely like the quotation Walton gives to Herbert about "spiritual Conflicts". Neither does Nicholas Ferrar in his preface to *The Temple*, which instead refers to the poems as providing evidence that God called Herbert to the priesthood. However, Walton had a vested interest in a Herbert who had written purely private, devotional verse. If this account can be recognized as the untrustworthy testimony that it is, modern critics will be able to evaluate more directly those poems by Herbert that respond to public controversies, reply to the poetry of literary coteries, and seek to promote worldwide Protestantism.[39]

II. The poetry of Grace

There are some topics and issues that "The Church" shares with Arminianism: the stone altar in the first poem, the emphasis on confession and the sacraments, the importance of the liturgy and the church calendar, the sense of reverence owed to the church and priesthood.[40] We also find in the sequence as well as *The Country Parson* warnings against theological controversy that are reminiscent of comments by those in the Laudian regime.[41] Herbert's efforts to restore Leighton Ecclesia and the rectory and church at Bemerton could have been inspired by Charles' proclamation in October 1629 that "churches and chapels" be restored.[42] At times Herbert seems to be at work to reveal points of unity between differing factions (see discussion of "The Altar", Chapter 3, and "The Windows", below). In most of these cases, however, Herbert is guided by the same views that determined *Musae Responsoriae* in 1620–21: a combination of conformity to the "sacred ritual" of the church and a commitment to Calvinist theology.[43] In his English lyrics, Herbert maintained his strong aversion to Rome and a fascination for the dynamics of salvation by grace alone.

"The Holdfast" may be the exemplary poem on this issue, since it both sums up the teaching on grace in the first poems in *The Temple* (see Chapter 3) and uses the sonnet form to make this point (see Chapter 1). Sacred love appears as an unnerving process of "letting go":

> I threatned to observe the strict decree
> > Of my deare God with all my power & might.
> > But I was told by one, it could not be;
> Yet I might trust God to be my light.
> Then I will trust, said I, in him alone.
> > Nay, ev'n to trust in him, was also his:
> > We must confesse that nothing is our own.
> Then I confesse that he my succour is:
> But to have nought is ours, not to confesse
> > That we have nought. I stood amaz'd at this,
> > Much troubled, till I heard a friend expresse,
> That all things were more ours by being his.
> > What Adam had, and forfeited for all,
> > Christ keepeth now, who cannot fail or fall.

As Fish makes clear in his discussion of this poem, the speaker holds fast to a belief that he can contribute to the process of salvation, but finds instead Christ as holdfast, the only possible means by which salvation can be certain.[44] The speaker's threatning in the first line recalls the imagery of competitive battle in "The Thanksgiving" and "The Reprisal", and hints at a problematic self-assertion implicit in the doctrine of salvation by merit. The quatrains pull together the speaker's plan of action, but it dissolves in the next few lines. The speaker attempts in each case to be as moral as he can, but he finds that human goodness is beside the point. Although the speaker uses the terms of sacred love, "my deare God", trusting "in him alone", "my succour", such devotion is unhelpful. In a reference perhaps aimed at the Arminians, the speaker learns that confession is not a measure of obedience, but an acknowledgment of powerlessness. Declarations of commitment, human strategies, expressions of love all are exposed as forms of possessiveness. The "friend" breaks in, as would an influx of grace: meaning comes from outside the soul. The couplet, often reserved for the poet's summation, appears here as the words of another.

"Dialogue" approaches grace not from the perspective of the speaker's virtue but his vice. The speaker is close to despair. Nevertheless, the poem suggests that a sense of unworthiness is similar to a sense of personal merit: both obscure the significance of the crucifixion:

> Sweetest Saviour, if my soul
> > Were but worth the having,
> Quickly should I then controll
> > Any thought of waving.
> But when all my care and pains
> Cannot give the name of gains
> To thy wretch so full of stains,
> What delight or hope remains?
>
> *What, Child, is the ballance thine,*
> > *Thine the poise and measure?*
> *If I say, Thou shalt be mine;*
> > *Finger not my treasure.*
> *What the gains in having thee*
> *Do amount to, onely he,*
> *Who for man was sold, can see;*
> *That transferr'd the'accounts to me.*
>
> But I can see no merit,
> > Leading to this favour:

So the way to fit me for it
    Is beyond my savour.
So the reason then is thine;
So the way is none of mine:
I disclaim the whole designe:
Sinne disclaims and I resigne.

That is all, if that I could
    Get without repining;
And my clay, my creature, would
    Follow my resigning:
That as I did freely part
With my glorie and desert,
Left all joyes to feel all smart – –
    Ah! no more: thou break'st my heart.

The poem represents salvation as a legal and financial agreement: given the speaker's inability to pay the wages of sin, he considers waiving his claim to redemption. Several words in the poem refer to renouncing a legal contract: wave or waive, disclaim, resign. Christ's part in the dialogue, however, reveals that human measures of evaluation cannot account for the covenants made possible by the crucifixion: "*that transferr'd th'accounts to me.*" God not man holds the scales and weights (the balance, poise, and measure, 9–10) that determine the value of the soul. In the first stanza, the speaker is overwhelmed by a sense of unworthiness. By the third stanza, this has developed into a refusal to participate in a "design" or agreement whose contours he cannot understand and which is not of his own making. The poem reveals the psychology of merit (17): the attempt to earn one's salvation and the despair that results from the effort is close to a form of willfulness. Christ illuminates this obstinacy through a contrast between resigning as renunciation and as yielding. The speaker cannot imitate Christ in his virtuous act of sacrifice, but the speaker can "follow" Christ's willingness to yield up his "glorie and desert". For Christ, this required God to suffer the humiliations of man; for the speaker, it means giving up the desire to see his way clear to salvation through righteous works. Like "The Altar", the speaker's broken heart in the last line is a sign of progress.

"Redemption" again uses the sonnet to explore Calvinist theology. Like "The Holdfast" and "Dialogue", the primary drama in the poem is the shock of the speaker at the truth of the crucifixion. Herbert's use of the sonnet for such matters suggests that his sense of "sacred love" included more than the commitment to write religious love poetry expressed in the sonnets "Love" I and II. Rather God initiates the deepest forms of this love. Walton's claim that the poems portray the private "Conflicts" between God and Herbert is countered by the relationship between this speaker and Christian history: he represents mankind in general in the movement from the Old Testament to the New:

> Having been tenant long to a rich Lord,
>> Not thriving, I resolved to be bold,
>> And make a suit unto him, to afford
> A new small-rented lease, and cancell th'old.
> In heaven at his manour I him sought:
>> They told me there, that he was lately gone
>> About some land, which he had dearly bought
> Long since on earth, to take possession.
> I straight return'd, and knowing his great birth,
>> Sought him accordingly in great resorts,
>> In cities, theatres, gardens, parks, and courts:
> At length I heard a ragged noise and mirth
>> Of theeves and murderers: there I him espied,
>> Who straight, *Your suit is granted,* said, & died.

The sonnet establishes, then demolishes an analogy between God and an aristocratic Lord. The speaker as tenant acts on his status expectations: he takes his suit to the manor house and later seeks the Lord in "great resorts". The speaker finds him instead in a "ragged" scene that conflates Christ's dining among "publicans and sinners" with his crucifixion between two thieves. The tenant hopes simply for some assistance on his "lease", but finds before speaking that the suit kills his Lord. He is a murderer as well as those surrounding Christ: all depend on the grace of the crucifixion rather than any social status, human virtue, or industrious effort.

The terms of the "small-rented lease", the new testament, exchange the death of God for the thriving of the speaker. His original complacency may be followed by burdensome guilt as well as the recognition of his devastating ignorance. In all of these poems, and particularly in "Redemption", the doctrine of merit is exposed as a form of blind egotism.

Arminians sought to keep predestination out of the sermons of the church because it rendered obedience to church authority and ritual insignificant to salvation. Herbert refers briefly to predestination in "The Thanksgiving", and addresses the issue in "The Watercourse":

> THou who dost dwell and linger here below,
>   Since the condition of this world is frail,
> Where of all plants afflictions soonest grow;
> If troubles overtake thee, do not wail:
>   For who can look for lesse, that loveth $\begin{cases} \text{Life?} \\ \text{Strife?} \end{cases}$ 5
>
> But rather turn the pipe and waters course
> To serve thy sinnes, and furnish thee with store
> Of sov'raigne tears, springing from true remorse:
> That so in purenesse thou mayst him adore,
>   Who gives to man, as he sees fit, $\begin{cases} \text{Salvation.} \\ \text{Damnation.} \end{cases}$ 10

This poem has been used to prove Herbert's Arminianism as well as his Calvinism.[45] Both interpretations are possible, because, whereas God is given utter power over election in the last line, man is given the ability to "turn the pipe, and waters course", by using tears for remorse over sins rather than grieving over afflictions. The poem leaves open the possibility that man's "pureness" can influence God's choice.

It would be wise to approach the poem not as evidence of a theological position, but rather as Herbert's effort to use the Arminian controversy to explore a deeper issue: repentance. The poem implies that, whatever one's views on predestination, humans need to stop complaining about their lot and start confronting their own vices. Herbert includes himself, given his five poems entitled "Affliction". Like "The Altar", the poet seeks out common ground in the poem in order to establish the deeper truths of regeneration.

That said, the poem bases its account of repentance on Calvinism. Jeanne Hunter Clayton has demonstrated that Herbert depends on water imagery used by Calvin (and adopted by Preston and Sibbes) to represent the power of grace and the freeing effects of predestination: "We shall never be clearly persuaded, as we ought to be, that our salvation flows from the wellspring of God's free mercy until we come to know of his eternal election, which illuminates God's grace by this contrast: that he does not indiscriminately adopt all into hope of salvation but gives to some what he denies to others ... in his outward Word, God may sufficiently witness his secret grace to us, provided the pipe, from which the water abundantly flows out for us to drink, does not hinder us from according due honor to the fountain. ..."[46] The fountain refers to God and Christ, whereas the pipe represents the "outward Word" and, for Preston, the sacraments, which direct grace toward man. From this perspective, the poem's command to "turn the pipe and water's course" means moving from self-oriented tears to the wellspring of grace. "Sov'raigne tears, springing from true remorse" are also part of what God "gives to man as he sees fit." The "pureness" that results refers not so much to human perfection as it does to gratitude rather than resentment over afflictions, and perhaps over predestination itself: "That so in pureness thou mayst him adore."

The shape of "The Water-course" emphasizes choice, but human choices turn out to be significantly restricted. The reader is taught to turn the water-course of tears away from grieving about troubles to remorse for sins, and God chooses between salvation and damnation for each soul, but the first double ending is in no way so clear (5). Taking afflictions properly may result in a love of "life" rather than "strife", but here as in other Herbert poems, loving the strife is also recommended: "Strive in this, and love the strife" ("The Banquet", 54). Loving the strife would not be the opposite of loving life but the same thing. The poem suggests that human choices are limited, that God "gives to man as he sees fit" not only salvation or damnation, but also afflictions and strife. Man's choice lies only in the ability to use each situation as an opportunity for repentance.

A water-course is defined by the *OED* as "a stream of water, a river or brook; also an artificial channel for the conveyance of water." Herbert clearly has in mind an artificial course that moves through a pipe. Through this reference he invokes the array of techniques introduced in the seventeenth century for the improvement of landed estates, including "drowning or draining" the grounds, as well as enclosure. Herbert explicitly praises these methods in *The Country Parson* (275) and through his translation of Cornaro's *Treatise of Temperance and Sobrietie* (301–2). Drowning the grounds had been put into practice on the Earl of Pembroke's estate in the seventeenth century, and was used during Herbert's residence at Bemerton. "The Water-course" forces us to reassess the conclusion, offered in the analysis of "Redemption" above, that Herbert finds no connection between the divine Lord and an aristocratic lord. Although man has some ability to "turn the pipe" and respond properly to afflictions, the maker of the pipe and the source itself for the water remains God alone. This suggests that at times Herbert imagines God according to the model of the improving landlord.[47]

The poetry of grace takes an autobiographical turn in "The Pearl" and "The Posie", although these poems never provide the "picture" into Herbert's soul that Walton desires. In "The Pearl. Matt. 13:45," the speaker is based on the merchant in the Biblical parable who sells all that he has to buy the pearl of great price, the kingdom of heaven. This speaker however is an upper-class man trained at the University and in the rituals of courtesy, like Herbert. Walton uses "The Pearl" as evidence that Herbert gave up his worldly ambitions to join the ministry.[48] But the poem was probably written long before he became a minister. Fish reads the poem as he does "The Holdfast" or "Dialogue", as dramatizing the education and transformation of a speaker.[49] As in "Dialogue", the speaker finds that "the way is none of mine" – a commitment to God is not a matter of choice or enlightened intelligence, but the effect of grace:

> I know the wayes of Learning; both the head
> And pipes that feed the presse, and make it runne;
> What reason hath from nature borrowed,
> Or of it self, like a good huswife, spunne
> In laws and policie; what the starres conspire,
> What willing nature speaks, what forc'd by fire;
> Both th' old discoveries, and the new-found seas,
> The stock and surplus, cause and historie:

All these stand open, or I have the keyes:
>   Yet I love thee.

I know the wayes of Honour, what maintains
The quick returns of courtesie and wit:
In vies of favours whether partie gains,
When glorie swells the heart, and moldeth it
To all expressions both of hand and eye,
Which on the world a true-love-knot may tie,
And bear the bundle, wheresoe're it goes:
How many drammes of spirit there must be
To sell my life unto my friends or foes:
>   Yet I love thee ...

I know all these, and have them in my hand:
Therefore not sealed, but with open eyes
I flie to thee, and fully understand
Both the main sale, and the commodities;
And at what rate and price I have thy love;
With all the circumstances that may move:
Yet through these labyrinths, not my groveling wit,
But thy silk twist let down from heav'n to me,
Did both conduct and teach me, how by it
>   To climbe to thee.   (1–20, 31–40)

Each of the first two stanzas includes images of complexity representing the intricacies of worldliness: "the head/ And pipes that feed
the presse", the "laws and policie" that reason has spun and the
"true-love-knot" that courtiers tie upon the world.[50] Each stanza
declares the speaker's ability to fully comprehend and maneuver
within these complexities, as well as the speaker's choice to love
God instead. The last stanza undermines these declarations and
their trust in the power of human choice through its own image of
intricacy, the labyrinth, which the speaker now admits he escaped
only through divine artfulness – the "silk twist" designed by grace.
Like "The Holdfast" and "Dialogue", the poem exposes belief in
one's own merit as blindness.

Both stanzas use details linked with Herbert's own experience.
The "head", "pipes" and "presse" in the first stanza conflate the

image of the winepress with the university press; publication is associated with the political essays and scientific discoveries of Bacon (7). The second stanza describes the rituals of courtesy outlined in "The Church-porch", particularly in terms of "the quick returns" of conversation and its effect on one's public reputation (stanzas 49–59). Is Herbert representing himself in the speaker?

He clearly wants the merchant's commercial wisdom ("the main sale, and the commodities ... the rate and price") to be linked with upper-class forms of expertise. Both are revealed to be inadequate in negotiating the movement from worldly success to spiritual dedication. It is probable that the theology of grace operated for Herbert in just this way, as a rebuke to the claims of upper-class mastery, especially any assertion that native or learned wit could control the shape of one's life. But this would have been a religious truth for him throughout his life, not just in 1624 and after.[51] The poem suggests that those who deal in "the wayes of Honour" go wrong when they tie a "true-love-knot" on the world, not when they participate in the world in any way. The poem may in fact be more like "Redemption" than autobiography in that it brings to life a Biblical passage through a fictional speaker. It would be a mistake to assume, as Walton does, that this poem records Herbert's complete withdrawal from the rituals of courtesy or the academy.

"The Posie" is a more explicitly autobiographical poem, yet still curiously indirect. Like the poems discussed above, the theology of grace is used to qualify human claims to virtue, ability, and value. It uses a motto or "posie" identified by Herbert's friends as his own: "Lesse than the least/ Of all Gods mercies." Using testimony from Arthur Woodnoth, Nicholas Ferrar writes in "The Printers to the Reader": "We conclude all with his own Motto, with which he used to conclude all things that might seem to tend any way to his own honour: *Lesse than the least of Gods mercies*" (3).[52] The poem identifies the "wayes of Honour" relevant here as the upper-class rituals of poetry itself:

> Let wits contest,
> And with their words and posies windows fill:
> *Lesse then the least*
> *Of all thy mercies*, is my posie still.

This on my ring,
This by my picture, in my book I write:
Whether I sing,
Or say, or dictate, this is my delight.

Invention rest,
Comparisons go play, wit use thy will:
Lesse than the least
Of all Gods mercies, is my posie still.

This motto creates a "posie" of grace because, as a quote from the Bible, it renounces personal achievement to keep in view the significance of divine power. The passage comes from the story of Jacob asking for God's help the night before meeting his brother Esau, whose birthright Jacob had stolen: "I am not worthy of the least of all the mercies, and all of the truth, which thou hast shewed unto thy servant; for with my staff I have crossed over this Jordan ..." (Gen. 32:10). The phrase refers indirectly to Herbert's use of Jordan in his lyrics to signal a commitment to religious rather than secular love poetry (see Chapter 1). In "Jordan" (II), originally entitled "Invention", the speaker must give up the belief that his elaborate poetic wit is more important than a simple expression of love. Like the "silk twist" of "The Pearl", and the "design" of Christ in "Dialogue", "The Posie" offers "*Gods mercies*" as the creative works deserving praise and honor rather than the work of the poet himself. Nevertheless, the poem does not renounce the upper-class rituals associated with poetry: "This on my ring,/ This by my picture, in my book I write:/ Whether I sing,/ Or say, or dictate, this is my delight" (5–8). This speaker, and, I suggest, Herbert himself, is represented as delivering his poetry through singing, speaking, or dictating, in all cases public activities.

III. Poems on employment

Scholars agree that the manuscript that eventually appeared as "B" was developed after the "W" manuscript, since the latter includes most of what is in "W" as well as several added poems.[53] Although there are a number of poems in "W" and "B" which express the desire for employment, "B" also includes poems that celebrate such employment. This shift from inactivity to fulfillment provides evidence that Herbert waited some significant amount of time before receiving the preferment he was seeking.[54]

The speaker in "Employment" (I), originally in "W", laments a life that is "barren to thy praise":

> If as a flowre doth spread and die,
>   Thou wouldst extend me to some good,
> Before I were by frosts extremitie
>   Nipt in the bud;
>
> The sweetnesse and the praise were thine;   5
>   But the extension and the room,
> Which in thy garland I should fill, were mine
>   At thy great doom.
>
> For as thou dost impart thy grace,
>   The greater shall our glorie be.   10
> The measure of our joyes is in this place,
>   The stuffe with thee.
>
> Let me not languish then, and spend
>   A life as barren to thy praise,
> As is the dust, to which that life doth tend,   15
>   But with delaies.
>
> All things are busie; onely I
>   Neither bring hony with the bees,
> Nor flowres to make that, nor the husbandrie
>   To water these.   20
>
> I am no link of thy great chain,
>   But all my companie is a weed.
> Lord, place me in thy consort; give one strain
>   To my poore reed.

Herbert uses the image of the flower frequently in "The Church" to represent spiritual and sometimes professional growth.[55] In this poem, the flower begins as part of God's "garland", a wreath made of flowers or leaves, worn on the head like a crown, and at times worn as a sign of distinction, like a royal diadem. Following the requirements of grace (9), the speaker affirms that the garland marks the value of God as victor, since the garland was worn by the winner of a contest, including competitions in poetry, and could represent glory itself (10). The speaker asks for a place in the garland, including "the extension and the room", that is, an occupation in space but also over time in a position or office, one meaning of "room" in the seventeenth century. As in "Dialogue" and other poems, the poem considers what is "thine" and "mine", (5,7), and seeks a resolution.

By the end of the poem, the image of the garland has radically changed. In stanza 5, the speaker widens his view from the garland to a country landscape, but finds again that he has no role, either as flower, bee, or farmer. Finally the status implications hidden by the garland and country imagery break out: "I am no link of thy great chain,/ But all my companie is a weed." Hierarchy intrudes, and the speaker's willingness to be simply a flower becomes questionable. The weed is disturbing in that it is unprofitable, and thus the poem alludes to the doctrine of vocation as well as the national program against idleness. But the weed is also distasteful because it ruins the elegance of God's world, and offends the speaker's status expectations about his appropriate "companie." The last lines of the poem seem to recognize this problem about status, and seek a more trustworthy form of humility, one that acknowledges the desire and complexity of human consciousness: "Lord, place me in thy consort; give one strain/ To my poore reed."[56] These lines acknowledge the drive to achieve glory as a poet, implicit in the image of the garland. The speaker becomes the pastoral piper, poor in abilities but capable of improvement, and contributing to a larger harmony.

"Employment" (II) operates at a higher speed. This speaker has no patience for inactivity or complaint because his goal is "business":

> He that is weary, let him sit.
> > My soul would stirre
> And trade in courtesies and wit,
> > Quitting the furre
> To cold complexions needing it.   5

Man is no starre, but a quick coal
          Of mortal fire:
Who blows it not, nor doth controll
          A faint desire,
Lets his own ashes choke his soul.   10

When th'elements did for place contest
          With him, whose will
Ordain'd the highest to be best;
          The earth sat still,
And by the others is opprest.   15

Life is a businesse, not good cheer;
          Ever in warres.
The sunne still shineth there or here,
          Whereas the starres
Watch an advantage to appeare.   20

Oh that I were an Orenge-tree,
          That busie plant!
Then should I ever laden be,
          And never want
Some fruit for him that dressed me.   25

But we are still too young or old;
          The Man is gone,
Before we do our wares unfold:
          So we freeze on,
Untill the grave increase our cold.   30

This poem rather uncharacteristically celebrates the desire "to be highest" in God's great chain of being. Man is "no starre", but he can imitate the stars by watching "for an advantage" (6, 20). By blowing on the "quick coal/ Of mortal fire", man can rise to the heights of achievement and avoid the failure of the earth, whose inactivity ensured that it would fall to the lowest place among those four elements believed to make up all things in the natural world: fire, air, water, and earth. The speaker's desire to ascend upward through "business" is represented in the poem as trading in "courtesies and wit", exactly the kind of activity that the gentle-man-merchant gives up in "The Pearl".

Herbert was himself hesitant about the celebration of business in this poem, since the image of the orange tree (in "B") replaces that of a bee mounting up "by degrees" (in "W"). The orange tree solves the problem about aggressive competition in the poem because it is continually fruitful, but never "highest". Being "dressed" by God (25) combines the pruning necessary for abundant fruit and the correction appropriate for a sinner. It is difficult to avoid the conclusion that the revisions were corrections in themselves, meant to weed out inappropriate energies.

"Affliction" (I) is a poem spun out of Herbert's life, although perhaps not directly autobiographical. It mentions vulnerability to sickness, the death of friends, and the life of the "gown", referring both to the university and the church. At issue here, as in the "Employment" poems, is the desire is to come to fruition both professionally and spiritually.[57] The speaker begins happily enough in his service to God, but this "world of mirth" is replaced by a "world of strife":

> When first thou didst entice to thee my heart,
> 　　　　I thought the service brave:
> So many joyes I writ down for my part,
> 　　　　Besides what I might have
> Out of my stock of naturall delights,
> Augmented with thy gracious benefits.
>
> I looked on thy furniture so fine,
> 　　　　And made it fine to me:
> Thy glorious houshold-stuffe did me entwine,
> 　　　　And 'tice me unto thee.
> Such starres I counted mine: both heav'n and earth
> Payd me my wages in a world of mirth.
>
> What pleasures could I want, whose King I served,
> 　　　　Where joyes my fellows were?
> Thus argu'd into hopes, my thoughts reserved
> 　　　　No place for grief or fear.
> Therefore my sudden soul caught at the place,
> And made her youth and fiercenesse seek thy face. (1–18)

The speaker begins by representing his original assurance that a dedication to God will be modeled on service to a king or aristocrat. Like the "great man" and his estate, the speaker's God had "glorious houshold-stuffe" and abundantly compensated his servants with "brave" or splendid finery. The speaker also enjoyed the benefits of both religious grace and natural "stock" (5–6); perhaps the advantages of his upper-class family seemed to easily blend with the grandeur of his new "master". Throughout these stanzas, the speaker implies that he was misled – he never realized the implications of the service he embraced with "youth and fiercenesse". Like many other speakers in Herbert's poetry, he discovers that "the way is none of mine":

> My flesh began unto my soul in pain,
>> Sicknesses cleave my bones;
> Consuming agues dwell in ev'ry vein,
>> And tune my breath to grones.
> Sorrow was all my soul; I scarce beleeved.
> Till grief did tell me roundly, that I lived.
>
> When I got health, thou took'st away my life,
>> And more; for my friends die:
> My mirth and edge was lost; a blunted knife
>> Was of more use than I.
> Thus thinne and lean without a fence or friend,
> I was blown through with ev'ry storm and winde.
>
> Whereas my birth and spirit rather took
>> The way that takes the town;
> Thou didst betray me to a lingring book,
>> And wrap me in a gown.
> I was entangled in the world of strife,
> Before I had the power to change my life. (25–42)

The afflictions of sickness and the death of friends are joined here with an even more disturbing awareness that the power of choice the speaker thought he was exercising has now been undermined. Whether or not he ever exercised that power, given the enticements of his master, now he is caught in "the world of strife". The speaker's sense of mastery seems linked with his "birth". As he loses "the way" associated with his family, he no longer determines his own direction. One wonders what exactly constitutes "the world of strife", but it seems related to the speaker's unwilling engagement with the "gown", both membership in the university and the clergy. Perhaps "strife" refers to the confrontation with sin required of the clergy but not those of upper-class birth or high secular office. The "book" at issue implies academic study, but also the Bible. Its description as "lingring" implies that his studies have not been rewarding. The word was often used to describe disease or poison, as if study itself was like a slow death. The speaker ends the poem wondering about his future and hoping for employment:

> Now I am here, what thou wilt do with me
> > None of my books will show:
> I reade, and sigh, and wish I were a tree;
> > For sure then I should grow
> To fruit or shade: at least some bird would trust
> Her houshold to me, and I should be just.[58]
>
> Yet, though thou troublest me, I must be meek;
> > In weaknesse must be stout.
> Well, I will change the service, and go seek
> > Some other master out.
> Ah my deare God! though I am clean forgot,
> Let me not love thee, if I love thee not. (55–66)

In the penultimate stanza, the speaker seems resigned and puzzled: "I reade, and sigh, and wish I were a tree." This line is both realistic and a joke on himself. The image of the tree appears, as it does in "Employment" (II), to express the desire for fruition, but in this poem, the speaker seems quite aware of its peculiar humility. He rebels against it in the last stanza by threatening to "change the service", only to recognize how inadequate the analogy of master and servant really is in representing commitment to an omnipotent deity. Finally he asks to be released from the affliction of being "chosen".

The above poems are included in the earlier "W" manuscript. Those discussed below voice similar desires and frustrations about employment, but they appear in the later "B" manuscript.

"Submission", "The Answer", and "The Quip" imply that Herbert's studies were indeed "lingring."

"Submission" considers again the relationship between grace and hierarchy in the speaker's career. Although the speaker assumes that appointment to a great place would display God's power most effectively, he confronts again the mysterious contours of God's "designe":

> But that thou art my wisdome, Lord,
>   And both mine eyes are thine,
> My minde would be extreamly stirr'd
>   For missing my designe.
>
> Were it not better to bestow   5
>   Some place and power on me?
> Then should thy praises with me grow,
>   And share in my degree.
>
> But when I thus dispute and grieve,
>   I do resume my sight,   10
> And pilfering what I once did give,
>   Disseize thee of thy right.
>
> How know I, if thou shouldst me raise,
>   That I should then raise thee?
> Perhaps great places and thy praise   15
>   Do not so well agree.
>
> Wherefore unto my gift I stand;
>   I will no more advise:
> Onely do thou lend me a hand,
>   Since thou hast both mine eyes.   20

If both "The Pearl" and "Submission" can be considered autobiographical, then the "sale" of all that the gentleman-merchant had did not remove from him the desire for a great place. Rather both poems refer to a decision to serve God rather than Mammon, and a gift ("Submission", 11, 17) to God of power over the speaker's life, including his ability to see and choose his way. "Disseize" (12) has the meaning of rob, but also to dispossess a person of his rightful estates. As in many Herbert poems, commitment to God implies yielding up ownership of the soul. Nevertheless, at this point, the speaker still believes that an appointment with some degree of honor associated with it (8) would be the most effective means of serving God. Unlike the speaker in "Affliction" (I), however, he recognizes that he actually has no say in the matter, and may be quite incorrect in his assessment: "How know I, if thou shouldst me raise,/ That I should then raise thee?/ Perhaps great places and thy praise/ Do not so well agree" (13–16).

"The Answer" and "The Quip" dramatize a speaker vulnerable to upper-class condemnations of him for an unfulfilled career. Oley tells us that one of Herbert's colleagues indeed felt that he "did not manage his brave parts to his best advantage and preferment, but lost himself in a humble way."[59] In both poems, the speakers lament such attacks, and create a defense through contemplating the intervention of grace. "The Answer" uses the sonnet form to develop and then undermine the reader's expectations for a clear conclusion in the couplet:

> My comforts drop and melt away like snow:
> I shake my head, and all the thoughts and ends,
> Which my fierce youth did bandie, fall and flow
> Like leaves about me: or like summer friends,
> Flyes of estates and sunne-shine. But to all,
> Who think me eager, hot, and undertaking,
> But in my prosecutions slack and small;
> As a young exhalation, newly waking,
> Scorns his first bed of dirt, and means the sky;
> And settling to a cloud, doth live and die
> In that dark state of tears: to all, that so
>> Show me, and set me, I have one reply,
>> Which they that know the rest, know more then I.

"Bandie" (3) uses the imagery of the tennis courts to evoke and then dispel the world of an upper-class young man talented at playful competition while serious in his pursuit of honor. That young man aimed toward the sky (8), as does the speaker in "Employment" (II), but now lingers in a "dark state of tears". His "settling" could suggest more hesitation and delay than the frustrated speaker of "Affliction" (I), but "The Answer" also implies that his "summer friends" abandoned him in response to a situation over which he had no control. The ending of the poem supports this view, since it offers no guilty explanation for his "state". Although the title of the poem leads us to expect a witty comeback bandied at the skeptics, the speaker responds out of the deepest ignorance about his future course, as if his own efforts had little to do with it. The "rest" (14) could refer to that future, or, leaving behind one's earthly life and reputation entirely, the eventual "rest" of salvation in heaven.

"The Quip" uses Herbert's life as material for a dramatic confrontation between a vulnerable silent speaker and the scorn of those surrounding him:

> The merrie world did on a day
> With his train-bands and mates agree
> To meet together, where I lay,
> And all in sport to geere at me.
>
> First, Beautie crept into a rose,
> Which when I pluckt not, Sir, said she,
> Tell me, I pray, Whose hands are those?
> *But thou shalt answer, Lord, for me.*
>
> Then Money came, and chinking still,
> What tune is this, poore man? said he:
> I heard in Musick you had skill,
> *But thou shalt answer, Lord, for me.*
>
> Then came brave Glorie puffing by
> In silks that whistled, who but he?
> He scarce allow'd me half an eie.
> *But thou shalt answer, Lord, for me.*
>
> Then came quick Wit and Conversation,
> And he would needs a comfort be,
> And, to be short, make an Oration.
> *But thou shalt answer, Lord, for me.*

> Yet when the houre of thy designe
> To answer these fine things shall come:
> Speak not at large; say, I am thine:
> And then they have their answer home.

As in "Dialogue" and "Submission", the poem creates a contrast between human expectations and "thy designe". The speaker in this poem, however, seems content to wait for future fulfillment, although he seems to expect rather a clear rebuke to his enemies. "I am thine" is the quip that God will deliver at some future time, and its wit combines God's claiming the speaker as His own (God will say, you are mine) and God promising that He belongs to the speaker as well (I am thine). The exact way in which this "answer" will be delivered remains almost as mysterious as "The Answer", particularly since "not at large" can mean not publicly. Perhaps only God and the speaker will enjoy this gentle witticism together in heaven. Nevertheless the possibility remains that the speaker hopes for a pointed rather than an extended response from God (another meaning of "not at large") in the shape of a public display that will put to rest the jeers of these unfriendly voices.

The poem uses as its refrain a line from Psalm 38 that suggests that the speaker's hostile audience includes family, friends, and enemies:

> My lovers and my neighbors did stand looking upon my trouble: and my kinsmen stood afar off ... For in thee, O Lord, have I put my trust: thou shalt answer for me, O Lord my God. I have required that they, even mine enemies, should not triumph over me (11–16).

The worldly figures that taunt the speaker refer to aspects of Herbert's life. "Beauty" sums up his decision not to write secular love poetry, "Money" derides his financial dependence on others throughout most of his life, "Glorie" condemns Herbert for his marginal gentility, "Wit and Conversation" embodies the pretensions of Herbert's life as Public Orator of Cambridge, including his claim to entertain the "great". The hopes placed on the forthcoming answer from God stem from self-knowledge as well as a powerful desire for compensation.

Unlike "W", the later "B" manuscript includes poems about
appointment to a position within the church. "The Crosse" is the
most explicit in this regard, and seems to comment directly on
many of the issues considered in the poems discussed above:

> What is this strange and uncouth thing?
> To make me sigh, and seek, and faint, and die,
> Untill I had some place, where I might sing,
>   And serve thee; and not onely I,
> But all my wealth and familie might combine   5
> To set thy honour up, as our designe.
>
>   And then when after much delay,
> Much wrastling, many a combate, this deare end,
> So much desir'd, is giv'n, to take away
>   My power to serve thee; to unbend   10
> All my abilities, my designes to confound,
> And lay my threatnings bleeding on the ground.
>
>   One ague dwelleth in my bones,
> Another in my soul (the memorie
> What I would do for thee, if once my grones   15
>   Could be allow'd for harmonie):
> I am in all a weak disabled thing,
> Save in the sight thereof, where strength doth sting.
>
>   Besides, things sort not to my will,
> Ev'n when my will doth studie thy renown: 20
> Thou turnest th'edge of all things on me still,
>   Taking me up to throw me down:
> So that, ev'n when my hopes seem to be sped,
> I am to grief alive, to them as dead.
>
>   To have my aim, and yet to be   25
> Further from it then when I bent my bow;
> To make my hopes my torture, and the fee
>   Of all my woes another wo,
> Is in the midst of delicates to need,
> And ev'n in Paradise to be a weed.   30

> Ah, my deare Father, ease my smart!
> These contrarieties crush me: these crosse actions
> Doe winde a rope about, and cut my heart:
>   And yet since these thy contradictions
> Are properly a crosse felt by thy Sonne,   35
> With but foure words, my words, *Thy will be done.*

The power of the crucifixion has driven the speaker to seek "some place, where I might sing,/ and serve thee." Like "Employment" (I), singing as a poet is conflated with serving in an appointment that honors God. The first two stanzas acknowledge that this pursuit of employment has been successful, but that nevertheless things did not turn out as the speaker imagined they would. This disappointment significantly does not include dissatisfaction at the lowliness of the post. Rather continuing sickness has made it impossible for the speaker to accomplish his "designe", a word important to any number of poems, including "Dialogue", "Submission", and "The Quip".

The speaker's desire for service is quite powerful. Meditation on the cross seems to have impelled him to "sigh, and seek, and faint, and die" – to dedicate his efforts to pursuing this course. Receiving a "place" only occurred after a significant period of time: "after much delay,/ Much wrastling, many a combate" (7–8). These lines do not explain who was responsible for the delay, although the speaker seems eager enough. The "wrastling" alludes not only to the agonistic struggles of "The Reprisal", but also the Biblical wrestling of Jacob with the angel of God before he meets Esau, also central to "The Posie". The word "wrestle" was used during this period to refer to striving earnestly with God in prayer, particularly in allusion to this story from the Bible.[60] The use of the word in line 8 represents the intense prayer used by the speaker in his seeking, as well as his belief that he had sufficiently subordinated his will to that of God in order to receive "this deare end".

The first stanza gives us some clues about the problems involved. The speaker had joyfully intended to use his "wealth and familie" to honor God. This suggests a happy resolution to the dilemmas about birth and status expressed in "Affliction" (I), "The Answer", and "The Quip". And yet the cross that moved this speaker is a "strange and uncouth thing." "Strange" and "uncouth" can mean alien and unfamiliar, and "uncouth" adds the meaning of indecorous, distasteful. The poem suggests that there is some kind of status dissonance between the "designe" of the speaker, especially given his family, and the requirements of the cross.

As the complaint of the speaker builds up, we find that it is the incongruity between the speaker's noble design and his experience of weakness that he finds particularly frustrating. Although he genuinely wants to "set thy honour up" and "study thy renown", he finds that God crosses his will: "taking me up to throw me down." The poem asserts that employment is no different from unemployment, since idleness is only replaced by sickness, but the speaker experiences this as status humiliation: it "is in the midst of delicates to need,/ And ev'n in Paradise to be a weed." Using the same image of the weed as "Employment" (I), this poem again coordinates fruitfulness with achieving upper-class decorum. "The Crosse" stresses the class implications of "weed" through the reference to "delicates", the fine viands at an aristocratic feast, luxuries rather than necessities.[61] Finally, in the last stanza, the speaker comes to realize that one meaning of the crucifixion is status dissonance: "And yet since these thy contradictions/ Are properly a crosse felt by thy Sonne,/ With but foure words, my words, *Thy will be done.*" What is "proper" takes on new meaning when applied to God the Father rather than one's "familie".

Hodgkins approaches "The Priesthood" as evidence that Herbert delayed for some years before being ordained as a priest.[62] Hodgkins argues that any delay was not out of secular ambition, but because Herbert was waiting for a divine call to the priesthood. It is difficult to coordinate "The Priesthood" with "The Crosse", as well as the other poems on employment discussed above, since these suggest that the speaker felt called to serve God early on in his religious life. Although "The Priesthood" voices strong apprehension about ordination, it also expresses the same desire for a place found in "The Crosse", and the same willingness to wait for the intervention of grace found in "Submission" and "The Quip":

> Blest Order, which in power dost so excell,
> That with th'one hand thou liftest to the sky,
> And with the other throwest down to hell
> In thy just censures; fain would I draw nigh,
> Fain put thee on, exchanging my lay-sword   5
> For that of th'holy Word.

But thou art fire, sacred and hallow'd fire;
And I but earth and clay: should I presume
To wear thy habit, the severe attire
My slender compositions might consume.
I am both foul and brittle; unfit
      To deal in holy Writ.

Yet have I often seen, by cunning hand
And force of fire, what curious things are made
Of wretched earth. Where once I scorn'd to stand,
That earth is fitted by the fire and trade
Of skilfull artists, for the boards of those
      Who make the bravest shows.

But since those great ones, be they ne're so great,
Come from the earth, from whence those vessels come;
So that at once both feeder, dish, and meat
Have one beginning and one finall summe:
I do not greatly wonder at the sight,
      If earth in earth delight. (1–24)

"Fain would I draw nigh," says the speaker, emphasizing his desire
to be a priest, as well as his fears of polluting the sacred order
through his own earthiness. As has been noted by several, Herbert
comes close to a Laudian account of the priesthood in this poem,
especially in his emphasis on its "power" (1). Nevertheless he also
stresses the "holy Word" (6,12), that is, the importance of Scripture
and of preaching, central to Calvinists, as well as the necessity of
grace, of being called by God rather than simply ordained by man.

As Schoenfeldt has demonstrated, power is a central issue in the
poem.[63] The first stanza focuses on the power of the priesthood to
save and damn, the difference between the "lay-sword", the temporal authority conferred through social status or state office, and
"that of th' Holy Word", the spiritual authority over souls and salvation. The next two stanzas consider the power of God's consuming
fire as the punishment for those unfit for sacred orders. "Slender
compositions" (10) can refer to states of body, or body and mind,
but also to writing, perhaps the sermons that the speaker feels
unprepared to compose, "unfit/ To deal in holy Writ". By the third
stanza, the poem is already developing a solution: God's fire cannot

only consume but also forge things anew, like the clay molded by potter in the Bible (Isa. 64:8, Jer. 18:6). Romans 9 is most applicable to the poem in the following verses: "Therefore hath he mercy on whom he will have mercy, and whom he will, he hardeneth ... Hath not the potter power over the clay, of the same lump can make one vessel unto honour, and another unto dishonour?" (18,21). So the speaker hopes and waits for the grace of reformation through the "cunning hand" of his Maker.

But the third and fourth stanzas include a form of social satire that is difficult to evaluate. The divine potter is compared to "skilfull artists" who create beautiful and "curious things" for their upper-class patrons. These things remain somewhat vague in this stanza, although "vessels" (pottery) for the "board" (table) are certainly included. But the language in the stanza also allows reference to buildings ("where once I scorn'd to stand"). Herbert imagines the finery of the aristocratic estate as the creation of the working classes, and suggests that great men primarily depend upon a façade for authority: "those/ who make the bravest shows."[64] The splendor of the great is exposed as fabrication, and the delight created through these "shows" is revealed as illusion, hiding the honest truth, that all aspects of the upper-class feast, including the people, are simply forms of dust: "So that at once both feeder, dish, and meat/ Have one beginning and one finall summe." This analysis seems to give the speaker the strength to imagine his own transformation:

> But th' holy men of God such vessels are,
> As serve him up, who all the world commands:
> When God vouchsafeth to become our fare,
> Their hands convey him, who conveys their hands.
> O what pure things, most pure must those things be,
> > Who bring my God to me!
>
> Wherefore I dare not, I, put forth my hand
> To hold the Ark, although it seem to shake
> Through th'old sinnes and new doctrines of our land.
> Onely, since God doth often vessels make
> Of lowly matter for high uses meet,
> > I throw me at his feet.

> There will I lie, untill my Maker seek
> For some mean stuffe whereon to show his skill:
> Then is my time. The distance of the meek
> Doth flatter power. Lest good come short of ill
> In praising might, the poore do by submission
>   What pride by opposition. (19–42)

Hodgkins notes that the poem is not only about power, but also about divine as opposed to human power.[65] Schoenfeldt is certainly right to claim that one is modeled on the other, given the line, "The distance of the meek/ Doth flatter power." But the speaker seems to need to get it clear for himself that the priesthood deals not primarily with "inferior power", as he puts it elsewhere, not with earth but with spirit, the God "who all the world commands"(26). The Eucharist is represented as a feast that is no illusion or fabrication, and in which power can both save and damn, whether parishioner or priest: "When God vouchsafeth to become our fare,/ Their hands convey him, who conveys their hands./ O what pure things, most pure must those things be,/ Who bring my God to me!" (27–30). Hands figure throughout the poem, both the hands of the priest (2, 28), of the skillful artist (13), or the well-intentioned Uzzah trying to steady the Ark as it travels in a cart drawn by oxen, but dying in the process (31). Herbert refers to the Biblical story (II Sam. 6:6), in which God kills the do-gooder, to distinguish again between pure hands and those motivated by merely human goodness. This motive is not enough, the speaker implies, even if one intends to help a church shaking "through th'old sinnes and new doctrines of the land." "New" could mean the reformation itself, but also the Arminianism and the Puritanism that developed because of it. Arminianism emphasized merit and obedience to church authorities rather than grace or predestination. This poem however insists on the power of God to "make one vessel unto honour, and another unto dishonour." However, the poem could also refer to separatists who claimed to be called to the ministry without institutional ordination. The speaker's response to the story of Uzzah is not only to ask to be reformed, but to keep the distance that Uzzah did not preserve between the holy and the human: "Onely, since God doth often vessels make/ Of lowly matter for high uses meet,/ I throw me at his feet" (34–36). Not touching God or the Ark until his hands are purified through grace seems to be of signal importance to the speaker. The poem may rebuke the Laudian reformers for their emphasis on the domesticated holiness of church ceremony as opposed to a Calvinist sense of God's fierce holiness obtainable only through grace. However the poem also rebukes a separatist or puritan lack of respect for the clerical orders.

The last few lines of the poem are curious, and have been interpreted in a variety of ways: "The distance of the meek/ Doth flatter power. Lest good come short of ill/ In praising might, the poore do by submission/ What pride by opposition." Hodgkins interprets "pride" as describing the act of Uzzah, who did not trust God's power in caring for the Ark. Thus the speaker rebukes his self-important desire to act as savior of the church. Schoenfeldt finds the "ill" to be courtiers who flatter through self-abasement, which the speaker satirizes but also imitates for the sake of "good". Hutchinson reads "pride" as referring to "those great ones" of the third and fourth stanzas: "The modest by observing a respectful deference pay a better homage than the proud who seek to keep up their state by a rival magnificence" (534). It seems to me that the central issue remains different kinds of power, and "ill" and "pride" both refer to the aristocrats described in the third and fourth stanzas. The speaker clarifies at the beginning that he would like to move from temporal to spiritual authority, from "my lay-sword" to "that of th'Holy Word".[66] The sword was a sign of gentility, and the speaker recognizes the significance of the change of clothes that will be involved. Thus the "bravest shows" of the aristocracy are not foreign to the speaker but quite familiar. No doubt he has delighted in the aristocratic feast more than once, and learned there how to "flatter power". In fact, the speaker may be apprehensive about moving from temporal to spiritual authority, partly because he will have to exercise the power of the priesthood against those "great ones". This could explain the rather curious social satire in the poem, as if understanding the priesthood requires critiquing the aristocracy. The poem may be largely an exercise in contrasting these two kinds of power. In the poem, he develops his ability to see "the bravest shows" of aristocrats as attempts to praise earthly power as superior to spiritual (what pride does by opposition). Through his exaggerated subordination before God, he praises the power of grace as primary, since it alone can raise him or anyone else above "clay and earth".

The speaker of "Aaron" has moved beyond waiting for ordination. Yet this poem shares with "The Priesthood" a powerful sense of religious awe at the holiness of God, and an anxiety about approaching that holiness:

> Holinesse on the head,
> Light and perfections on the breast,
> Harmonious bells below, raising the dead
> To leade them unto life and rest:
> Thus are true Aarons drest.
>
> Profaneness in my head,
> Defects and darknesse in my breast,
> A noise of passions ringing me for dead
> Unto a place where is no rest:
> Poore priest thus am I drest.
>
> Onely another head
> I have, another heart and breast,
> Another musick, making live not dead,
> Without whom I could have no rest:
> In him I am well drest.
>
> Christ is my onely head,
> My alone onely heart and breast,
> My onely musick, striking me ev'n dead;
> That to the old man I may rest,
> And be in him new drest.
>
> So holy in my head,
> Perfect and light in my deare breast,
> My doctrine tun'd by Christ, (who is not dead,
> But lives in me while I do rest)
> Come people; Aaron's drest.

The poem maintains a sense of order through the set of rhymes repeated in every stanza: head, breast, dead, rest, drest. It is clear that the priesthood did not prevent Herbert from exercising his poetic skill, despite the stress on simplicity in the poetry of grace.

The order of the rhymes suggests as well the elegant order of Aaron's attire, ornate and curious, the work of the cunning workman, as described in Exodus 28. But the emphasis on externals, also important to contemporary debate about the surplice, is joined in the poem with a crucial consideration of the internal: the second stanza expresses the depths of despair, since the speaker's "profaneness" could again lead to his spiritual death (6–9).[67] It is in fact the soul that needs dressing, which can only occur through grace. The word "drest" unites clothing with correction, as it does in the revision to "Employment" (II). Hodgkins and Strier have suggested, in fact, that this poem could have been written by a Presbyterian, since it finally praises the "priesthood of all believers". But Guibbory accurately points out that the poem brings together the finery of the priest's clothes with the true Christian within.[68]

The poem explores the description of Aaron's garments in Exodus 28, as it seeks for their Calvinist meaning. The mitre worn on the head like a turban bore a plate of gold in which was written "HOLINESS TO THE LORD". This allowed Aaron to approach the Lord with the tainted gifts of the people (Ex. 28:38). The poem finds that the speaker has only "profaneness" in his head (6) until he turns to the people's true savior: "Christ is my onely head" (16). This rhyme expands its original meaning from the priest's mitred head to the master or head to whom the priest is subordinate, a master who is also the source for holiness and intelligence.

The breastplate of Aaron included the Urim and Thummin, material objects which represented "light and perfectnesse" according to Coverdale, and doctrine and truth, according to the Vulgate (*OED*). These allowed Aaron to "bear the judgment of the children of Israel on his heart before the Lord continually" (Ex. 28:30). The poem interprets this as requiring the priest to take religious doctrine to heart and live it for the sake of the people, teaching it through example. Given the speaker's "defects and darknesse" (7), only the love of Christ makes this possible: "my alone onely heart and breast" (17).

The "harmonious bells below" (3) were actually stitched on the bottom of Aaron's robe, and alerted the people to pray as the High Priest approached the Lord as their representative. The power of the Biblical Aaron is increased through linking him with Jesus, who was capable of "raising the dead/ To leade them unto life and rest." The poem also connects these figures to the English priest through the ringing of the parish bell, calling parishioners to a service that, the poem warns, can raise the dead literally and metaphorically, if the minister is prepared. This preparation is represented by the discords and harmonies of music, either the "noise of passions" within the speaker or "my doctrine tun'd by Christ" (8,23). Such tuning is only possible when the bell tolls for the speaker, "striking me ev'n dead", so he can be raised from the dead by Christ "new drest", as the new man (19). "My doctrine tun'd by Christ" becomes the harmony achieved within through grace as well as the expression of that internalized doctrine in the sermon.

"The Windows" again explores the relationship between the external things of the church and their internalized meaning. The issue was renewed in significance one month after Herbert became a priest when Henry Sherfield, a town official, broke a stained glass window in St. Edmund's, Salisbury, in October 1630. Bishop Davenant had refused to allow the parishioners to replace the worn-out window with plain glass. Davenant took Sherfield to the Star Chamber, and he was fined L500. The king however allowed the parishioners to replace the broken pane with the plain glass they desired in the first place.

As in several other poems, Herbert tries to find common ground between ceremonialists and iconoclasts. He seems most intent on strengthening the reverence of parishioners for the church through the holy life of the preacher. By making preaching central, Herbert supports the claims of Calvinists that Laud and the Arminians were giving priority to ceremony rather than the "Word" through their emphasis on "things indifferent", like the railed-off altar at the east end of the church or a stained-glass window, and through their restrictions on references to predestination in sermons. Also, unlike "Aaron", the poem seems unconcerned about the physical object, since it only appears as a metaphor for the effect of a minister's words. But there can be no doubt that the poem seeks to reinforce the power of the church and the priest. The reverence that Sherfield did not show toward the church is exactly the goal of the poem:

> Lord, how can man preach thy eternall word?
> He is a brittle crazie glasse:
> Yet in thy temple thou dost him afford
>   This glorious and transcendent place,
>   To be a window, through thy grace.   5

But when thou dost anneal in glasse thy storie,
   Making thy life to shine within
The holy Preachers; then the light and glorie
   More rev'rend grows, & more doth win:
   Which else shows watrish, bleak & thin.   10

Doctrine and life, colours and light, in one
   When they combine and mingle, bring
A strong regard and aw: but speech alone
   Doth vanish like a flaring thing,
   And in the eare, not conscience ring.   15

Words ringing in the conscience sound very much like the bells in "Aaron": "raising the dead/ To leade them unto life and rest" (3–4). In both poems, the power of the preacher's words depend on "doctrine tun'd by Christ", that is, the harmonizing of doctrine and life together. "The Windows" is also fundamentally interested in the power of grace, but for its public purposes, to create a "strong regard and aw" (13). Thus the poem doesn't address a literal stained-glass window, but it does make central the institutional "temple" (3), and the need to maintain respect for it among the church membership.

The speaker now has "a glorious and transcendent place" (4). Yet he remains "a brittle crazie glass", very like the "foul and brittle" speaker of "The Priesthood" (11) "Crazie" meant full of cracks or flaws: although the light of doctrine shines through the words of the preacher, it is distorted by the marks on the glass and deadened by its bleakness. Color brings out the radiance and vividness of the truth when, through grace, the minister makes Christ's experience his own. This internalizing process is not easy: the annealing used in making a stained-glass window suggests the burning, reforming fire of God the craftsman, important to "The Priesthood". This divine art working "within" the preacher brings the truth to life in his words. These words do not flare out or dazzle, and then vanish. Rather they speak to the conscience (9) and create "aw" (13), for God, one supposes, but also for the church. Certainly, Herbert is more concerned about the salvation of the parishioners than their obedience. Nevertheless it is difficult to imagine Sherfield breaking a stained-glass window with Aaron's bells tolling in his conscience.

IV. Poems on the church

"The British Church" and "Church-rents and schisms" were probably written later in Herbert's life since they are present in the "B"
manuscript but not in the earlier "W". Comparing these two later
poems is like analyzing the earlier *Musae Responsoriae* and "The
Church-militant" together: the same institution is described as
beautifully ordered and radically degenerated. I hope to show in
this final section that Herbert represents through this contrast the
ideal and the real, and that his ideal remained the same throughout his life. For Herbert, the English church provided the best
model for an imperial Protestantism to be established throughout
the world.

"The British Church" reproduces many aspects of *Musae
Responsoriae*, including the ideal of the middle way between the
corruption of Rome and the vulgarity of Puritanism. The English
church becomes the model for a civilized society:

> I joy, deare Mother, when I view
> Thy perfect lineaments and hue
> > Both sweet and bright.
> Beautie in thee takes up her place,
> And dates her letters from thy face,   5
> > When she doth write.
>
> A fine aspect in fit aray,
> Neither too mean, nor yet too gay,
> > Shows who is best.
> Outlandish looks may not compare: 10
> For all they either painted are,
> > Or else undrest.
>
> She on the hills, which wantonly
> Allureth all in hope to be
> > By her preferr'd,   15
> Hath kiss'd so long her painted shrines,
> That ev'n her face by kissing shines,
> > For her reward.

> She in the valley is so shie
> Of dressing, that her hair doth lie   20
>   About her eares:
> While she avoids her neighbours pride,
> She wholly goes on th'other side,
>   And nothing wears.
>
> But, dearest Mother, what those misse,   25
> The mean, thy praise and glorie is,
>   And long may be.
> Blessed be God, whose love it was
> To double-moat thee with his grace,
>   And none but thee.   30

Although it is conventional to claim that in his later years Herbert became less aggressive in his religious polemic, this poem suggests that Herbert's antagonism to Catholicism and Puritanism never diminished.[69] Both religions are described as "outlandish" (10) or foreign, and represented as potential invaders of a pure British soil. God has properly protected this insularity through a "double-moat", both grace and the sea (29). Although in his earlier work Herbert rebukes the Puritans as excessive for describing Rome as "the she-wolf of the Vatican brothel" (#30), his account of Catholicism here also links that church with the whore of Babylon, as he does in "The Church-militant" (211–220). *Musae Responsoriae* explicitly connected Puritanism with Scotland, since it answered Andrew Melville, but this poem unites England with Scotland through the term "British". Nevertheless, it remains possible that the naked woman representing the Calvinists in Geneva also represents the unruly Scots, still threatening from the north, especially given the phrase "so shie/ Of dressing," or correction. It is worthwhile to remember that the first time Herbert used this image for the Puritans, in a poem "On the use of rites", he associated nakedness with the primitive Britons invaded and ruled over by the Roman Julius Caesar. So England properly rules over the Scots, given their "barbariem patrum" or barbaric state (*Musae Responsoriae* #25: 11).

The reference to the church as "mother" was conventional for conformists during this period.[70] However, Heather Asals points out the similarity between the description of the church here and views about Magdalene Herbert.[71] In his funeral sermon, Donne commented, "Shee never diverted towards the *Papist*, in undervaluing the *Scripture*, nor towards the *Separatist*, in undervaluing the *Church*". As in her religion, so in her dress: "And for her Attire ... it was never *sumptuous,* never *sordid*: But always agreeable to her *quality*, and agreeable to her *company*."[72] In *Memoriae Matris Sacrum*, Herbert also stresses decorum in his mother: in her appearance ("She did not deck herself so grandly she/ Wasted time that glides away, nor did she/ Pile up her hair as high as pride," #2:10–12) and use of language ("beauteous the shell,/ Most beauteous the kernel,/ Thought and word exactly in accord" #2:36).[73] This also seems to be Herbert's model of beauty in the poem: "Beautie in thee takes up her place,/ And dates her letters from thy face,/ When she doth write" (3–6). This refers to the tradition of dating the New Year by the old calendar, beginning on March 25, Lady Day, or the Feast of the Annunciation of the Virgin. But these lines also imply that beautiful language takes its cue from the decorum of the British Church, never naked or overly artificial, but always "a fine aspect in fit aray."

The gender implications of the imagery in the poem conflate church ritual with the proper government of female sexuality. The Puritan church is "shie" but also resistant to discipline, slovenly and ignorantly stubborn in the refusal to be clothed. There is some suggestion that a church, like a woman, shows her obedience by yielding to the requirement to use her beauty to attract followers. Thus, unlike Herbert's mother, the Puritan church is not entirely socialized, since it refuses to be "agreeable" or pleasing. On the other hand, the Church of England arrays itself with "sacred ritual" in order to reveal its best advantages. But nakedness not only suggests unwillingness to please but also primitive and even dangerous immodesty, as it does in "On the use of rites": "they ... lay her, entirely/ Ignorant of clothing, bare to conquest/ By Satan and her enemies." Clothing a woman represents the protection of a developed ecclesiastical cultus, but also the civilizing process, sophisticated and intelligent in the use and defense of its resources. Simply put, the British Church is more advanced than the Puritan: "And Christ himself ... says that only England offers him a finished worship" [plenos ... cultus] (*Musae Responsoriae*, #39).

The Roman church has instead become decadent. This includes not only the prostitution of religion but the corruption of the process of appointment to office: "She on the hills, which wantonly/ Allureth all in hope to be/ By her preferr'd ..." The attractions of this church have become more important than its moral purity; it has become "wanton" in its seduction not only of followers but ambitious clergy. Herbert could be referring obliquely to the preferment policies of Laud and Charles I, since it is clear that the more English ministers preferred high church ritual, the more they were preferred into lucrative church offices. In any case, Herbert condemns excessive ritual as superstition: "She .../ Hath kiss'd so long her painted shrines,/ That ev'n her face by kissing shines,/ For her reward." This evokes Jesus' condemnation of those who pray or fast in public for "the glory of men" rather than for the rewards of God obtained by praying in secret:

> And when thou prayest, thou shalt not be as the hypocrites are: for they love to pray standing in the synagogues and in the corners of the streets, that they may be seen of men. Verily, I say unto you, They have their reward. But thou, when thou prayest, enter into thy closet, and when thou hast shut thy door, pray to thy Father which is in secret; and thy Father which seeth in secret shall reward thee openly. (Matt. 6:5–6)

Elaborate ritual like the use of the railed-in altar at the east end of the church may attract attention, but its superstitious elegance can never achieve the effects of honest prayer. Although the Puritan church is "undrest", shy of public appearances, and primitive, the Roman church is "painted", a fabricated culture with humanly constructed "shrines", having lost touch with authentic religion.

Although Herbert praises the British church, he implies that the two unwanted extremes could be just as present within England as without. These possibilities also underlie "Church-rents and schisms", which never identifies the church it considers, but allows its criticism to be applied both to the Christian church at home and abroad:

> Brave rose, (alas!) where art thou? in the chair
> Where thou didst lately so triumph and shine

A worm doth sit, whose many feet and hair
Are the more foul, the more thou wert divine.
This, this hath done it, this did bite the root   5
And bottome of the leaves: which when the winde
Did once perceive, it blew them under foot,
Where rude unhallow'd steps do crush and grinde
       Their beauteous glories. Onely shreds of thee,
       And those all bitten, in thy chair I see.   10

Why doth my Mother blush? Is she the rose,
And shows it so? Indeed Christs precious bloud
Gave you a colour once; which when your foes
Thought to let out, the bleeding did you good,
And made you look much fresher then before.   15
But when debates and fretting jealousies
Did worm and work within you more and more,
Your colour vaded, and calamities
       Turned your ruddie into pale and bleak:
       Your health and beautie both began to break.   20

Then did your sev'rall parts unloose and start:
Which when your neighbours saw, like a north-winde
They rushed in, and cast them in the dirt
Where Pagans tread. O Mother deare and kinde,
Where shall I get me eyes enough to weep,   25
As many eyes as starres? since it is night,
And much of Asia and Europe fast asleep,
And ev'n all Africk; would at least I might
       With these two poore ones lick up all the dew,
       Which falls by night, and poure it out for you!   30

Hutchinson provides the best starting point for an analysis of the poem: "The Church is figured as 'the rose of Sharon' (Song of Songs, ii, 1) in her *chair* of authority: schisms *within you* (l.17) harm the Church more than assaults from without (ll.13–15), which purge her of insincere adherents." Critics identify these schisms in opposite ways. For Guibbory, the source of dissent is the Puritans destroying the beauty of the ceremonial church (53), whereas for Hodgkins, the worm is the corruption of Laudian reform, destroying the

Elizabethan *via media* (1, 184). Although these issues are relevant, the poem requires a wider context in time and space, since this church existed before Christ, and its final goal is universal Christianity: "Indeed Christs precious bloud/ Gave you a colour once .../ ... much of Asia and Europe [is] fast asleep,/ and ev'n all Africk ..." (12–13, 26–28).

The poem refers to the true church in terms similar to "The Church-militant". In that poem, that church as "Spouse" began with the Hebrew patriarchs and moves over the ages toward the west, with an apocalyptic ending in the Americas. So "Church-rents and schismes" tells the history of the true church, and in fact tells it twice. The first stanza describes in imagery the "brave rose" bitten to pieces by the "worm" and scattered by the "winde" (6). The second and third stanzas narrate the history of Christ's sacrifice, which makes the church "look much fresher than before" (15), after which debates destroy this strength and unity, and "neighbors ... like a north-winde" scatter the parts (22). The foul "worm" with its "many feet and hair" is a disturbing image, partly because it reigns as authority, and partly because the image for the church is not only a rose, but also a woman, "my Mother" (11). We are meant to imagine not only a caterpillar eating the rose, but Satan as serpent, corrupting Eve again.

"Christ's precious bloud" (12) can refer to Christ's sacrifice as well as to the Protestant martyrs in England. Just as Christ brought the true church to life through his death, so Protestants willing to die for their faith revitalized the true church in England. Those responsible for the destructive "debates" (16) that followed include the Puritans. Herbert describes a Puritan as a "Schismatick" in *The Country Parson*. He also represents their vision of the church as "rude" and "unhallow'd" (8) in both "The British Church" and *Musae Responsoriae*. As Powers-Beck suggests, the "north-winde" (22) could refer to Scotland. But it would be unwise to single out the Puritans as the only offending party. The corrupting worm has "many feet", suggesting that all parts are responsible for the disunity. Also, no Puritan sat in the chair of authority in England. The poem indirectly attacks the church leadership that has allowed this disunity to occur. The foul worm in the chair of authority most closely resembles the figure of "Sinne" ruling the Roman church in "The Church-militant" (161–208); if so, the poem takes aim at the

Catholic church and criticizes Catholic influences in England. "Fretting jealousies" (26) could refer to the reformation, during which Rome refused to be reformed in order to maintain unity, but it also suggests the anxieties over preferment created by the Arminian party, uninterested in preserving the balance of the Jacobean church, in which clergy of all persuasions were promoted.

Like "The Church-militant", "Church-rents and schisms" associates the vitality of the church with the power of empire. The scattering of the true church sounds very much like the destruction of the Roman Empire by the northern barbarians: "Which when your neighbors saw, like a north-winde/ They rushed in, and cast ["your sev'rall parts] in the dirt/ Where Pagans tread" (12–14). Just as the barbarians destroyed the power and civilization of Rome, so "Pagans" threaten to crush the civilizing mission of the Church of England, which includes the conversion of the world. Although the poem focuses on the enemies within, it is also concerned about enemies without, like the Islamic nations or the "heathens" of other lands, who resist the missionary work of Christianity. Herbert suggests that the disunity of the church makes the international cause of spreading Protestantism to Asia, Europe, and Africa almost impossible.

Between the time of Herbert's celebration of international Protestantism in his Cambridge years and his ordination as a country parson in Bemerton, several new church-rents and schisms had occurred in England. Some of these, particularly the rise of the Arminian orthodoxy, had a direct effect on his career. Perhaps his optimism about the future of Protestantism had significantly dimmed since the time he wrote "To the Lady Elizabeth Queen of Bohemia". Nevertheless he still believed in the importance, if not the swift success, of a universal religion: "Thence, wheeling on, it compasse shall/ This, our great sublunary ball ... (II.7–12).

Afterword: *The Country Parson*

It is clear that several people around George Herbert during his Bemerton years felt he had renounced the pursuit of status and worldly honor. Arthur Woodnoth testifies as much when he urges his cousin Nicholas Ferrar not to dedicate *The Temple* to Edward, Lord Herbert of Cherbury and Castle Island, since a "title of Honour" is of no use in representing the value of "gods saynts". Woodnoth cites as his source a statement similar to a line from "The Posie": "less than the least of Gods mercyes was his motto." Doerksen argues convincingly that this letter from Woodnoth is the reason why Ferrar chose to write "The Printers to the Reader" rather than a dedication to Edward Herbert:[1]

> The dedication of this work having been made by the Authour to the *Divine Majestie* onely, how should we now presume to interest any mortall man in the patronage of it? ... We conclude all with his own Motto, with which he used to conclude all things that might seem to tend any way to his own honour; *Lesse then the least of Gods mercies.* (3–5)

This view of Herbert as renouncing status for spirituality corresponds with other evidence provided by those at Little Gidding. John Ferrar testified that Herbert wrote a letter to Nicholas of "free and Xtian council", in which he urges Ferrar "to attend to the great Christian duty of Mortification, & with true humble contempt of the world: not to be frighted with the suspitions, slanders & scornes which worldly persons would throw upon them" (577). This exhortation to resist the scorn of the worldly perhaps explains one of the more loaded sentences in another of Herbert's letters to Nicholas. Herbert thanks Ferrar for his help on rebuilding the Leighton church, and encourages him to continue to provide advice,

> I ... am so far from giving you cause, to apology, about your counseling me herein: that I take it exceeding kindly of you. I refuse not advice from the meanest, that creeps upon Gods earth, no not tho' the advice step so far, as to be reproof: much less can I disesteem it from you, whome I esteem to be God's faithfull & diligent Servant, not considering you any other wayes, as neyther I my self desire to be considered. Particularly, I like all your Addresses, & for ought I see, they are ever to be liked. (378)

Herbert rejects any status considerations as pertinent to his relationship with his "brother" Ferrar, and identifies both exclusively in terms of their religious commitment. Taken together this evidence could suggest that not only did Woodnoth and the Ferrar brothers think of Herbert as having renounced the possibility of promotion, but also that Herbert actually had done so. From this perspective, he used his motto, *"Lesse than the least of Gods mercies"*, to ensure his "true and humble contempt for the world".[2]

However, we have no conclusive proof that Herbert used this motto in his daily conversation rather than in "The Posie" alone. Woodnoth could have found the words in the poem, and chosen them as epitomizing the Herbert that he knew.[3] Nicholas may have been completely dependent on Woodnoth's words and the poem, not on any spoken words from Herbert. "The Posie" in fact represents the speaker as participating in a number of upper-class activities, including engraving "posies" on a ring, and singing and reciting his poetry. But the Ferrar brothers would value an image of Herbert that reproduced their own withdrawal from public life. The letters from Herbert to Nicholas indeed demonstrate that Herbert felt a special bond with Ferrar, but this might be grounded in their ordination within the church, not in any sense of retreat from the world. In the letter that John summarized, Herbert seems most interested in strengthening Ferrar's resistance to former colleagues who have contempt for gentlemen who choose to take orders: "not to be frighted with the suspitions, slanders & scornes which worldly persons would throw upon them." Herbert's letter about Leighton church rules out status but also suggests that Ferrar needed to be reassured on the subject of his "Addresses", as if Ferrar felt that he was not being properly deferential with one higher in rank and family connections. Herbert is quick to insist on his esteem for Ferrar, but not because of any meditative withdrawal. When Herbert considers Ferrar and himself only as "God's faithfull & diligent Servant[s]", it is most likely that he refers to their position within the church, not to any shared retreat from the world.

None of the evidence given above proves that Herbert had rejected the idea of promotion within the church. He is however very cautious on the subject. In "The Parson's state of Life", he considers promotion, "Ambition, or untimely desire of promotion to an higher state, or place, under colour of accommodation, or necessary provision, is a common temptation to men of any eminency, especially being single men" (238). Although married, Herbert warns against ambition as one aspect of his program of "Mortification" in a passage very similar to the letter that John Ferrar summarizes. This program was used to maintain "profound humility" and "exact temperance" in his life as parson (237). Nevertheless the passage rules out "untimely desire of promotion", not advancement of any kind. Herbert believed that God chose his ministers, and, therefore, God could just as easily place them in a higher position. Thus he describes the clergy in his letter in 1631 to Arthur Woodnoth:

> For any scruple of leaving your trade, throw it away ... to chuse a higher work, as God gives me higher thoughts, & to rise with his favours, can not but be not only allowable but commendable. The case of ministers and magistrates is another thing, the one are Gods servants, the other the commonwealths, & therefore not relinquishable without their masters consent ... (381).

Here, Herbert warns against leaving the ministry, not advancing within it. To be a minister to Herbert clearly meant to serve God, not man, but this leaves open the possibility that God's servant could "rise with his favours". "The Windows" in fact describes God as placing man in "this glorious and transcendent place" as a preacher. If we read this poem autobiographically, it is interesting that Herbert expresses no dissatisfaction with the position at Bemerton, nor does he do so anywhere else. "The Crosse" suggests that the speaker has been given a place where he can use "all my wealth and familie ... to set thy honour up ...". "The Parson's state of Life" describes men like Herbert as being in a position of "eminency" (238). It is worth remembering that his predecessor at Bemerton was promoted to become the Bishop of Bath and Wells.

Herbert may have felt that preferment was unlikely, given his record between 1624 and 1630. Nevertheless the possibility remains, as Cooley has claimed, that he prepared his pastoral manual *The Country Parson* not only for himself or posterity, but to announce his willingness to be considered for higher office. As many have argued, this manual does not accept Laudian policy or reform, and in many cases, rejects it. Therefore, I find it difficult to believe that advancement was Herbert's primary purpose in writing the manual. However, it is entirely reasonable to assume that, as Herbert spelled out his own beliefs on the duties of a minister, he believed that he might prove himself capable of higher duties.

When the manual was finally published, in 1652, it had received a Laudian makeover. Barnabas Oley published the work with a new title, "The Priest to the Temple". Doerksen has argued convincingly that Arminian anxieties prohibited the manual with its original title from earlier publication. Sir Robert Cooke described the book "stiled the Country Parson" in a 1641 letter to Sir Robert Harley that urges him to ensure that the manual be published. Cooke was Jane Herbert's second husband, and a puritan Parliamentarian along with Harley. Cooke tells of the difficulties Arthur Woodnoth had previously encountered in getting the book licensed: "he used some indeavors to get it allowed, but I conceived the booke to be too good for those times ..." Cooke probably refers to the period of "the high Laudian era", as Doerksen puts it, before Parliament was called in 1640. Cooke writes after the impeachment and execution of Stafford, and seems to believe that the licensers would receive the work more positively at this point. However Woodnoth had given the work to Richard Holdsworth, Master of Emmanuel College, who was at the time a moderate puritan, but soon became a royalist. Apparently a license could not be obtained, particularly given Cooke's condition for publication, "that it may be printed without any alteration of the Copie delivered by Mr. Woodnoth to

Dr Holdsworth." Oley seems to have rejected that condition in providing a new title in 1652, and, in 1671, in printing the work
without "The Author's Prayer before the Sermon" and "A Prayer
after Sermon". Doerksen describes these prayers as "fervent, evangel-
ical, and even predestinarian".[4] Oley's revisions to *The Country
Parson* paved the way for Walton's fabrication of Herbert as a
Laudian royalist completely absorbed in high-church ceremony.

As Veith and I have argued, *The Country Parson* maps out Herbert's
participation in the "Protestant ethic" as well as his engagement in
the world.[5] As in "The Church-porch", Herbert attacks idleness as
the "great and national sin of this Land" (274). He advocates work
in a calling for everyone: " ... every gift or ability is a talent to be
accounted for, and to be improved to our Masters Advantage. Yet is
it also a debt to our Countrey to have a Calling, and it concernes
the Common-wealth, that none should be idle, but all busied"
(274). He finds "intolerable" the "neglect" of those like himself,
"younger Brothers" in upper-class homes, who have not been prepared for a profession, which is "a shamefull wrong both to the
Common-wealth, and their own House" (277). He comments as well
on "generall ignominy" cast on his own profession, but urges ministers to fight it, "for that, where contempt is, there is no room for
instruction" (268). The manual itself is part of Herbert's plan to
improve his own talents to "feed my Flocke diligently and faith-
fully" (224), and each chapter records instructions on particular
duties. It is true that the work refers only very briefly to the Court
("as the eminent place both of good and ill") and to the House of
Commons and Lords: "there is no school to a Parliament" (277).
Nevertheless the manual considers rather fully the duties of
various callings in society, including the landed elite. As we would
expect, given Herbert's previous references to international
Protestantism, the Parson urges younger sons to find their vocation
overseas, "where can he busie himself better, then in those new
Plantations, and discoveryes, which are not only a noble, but also,
as they may be handled, a religious imployment" (278).

As many have argued, Herbert maintains his position as a conformist Calvinist in *The Country Parson*.[6] Despite the Laudian
emphasis on sacraments rather than the word, Herbert devotes a
long chapter to preaching, in which he describes a style similar to
that used in the poetry of grace, called the "character" of holiness.

Herbert clearly distinguishes this style from that of Arminians like Lancelot Andrewes. The chapter on preaching is the seventh, whereas the chapter on the sacraments in twenty-third, which also suggests the importance of the word to Herbert's ministry. "The Parson's Church" clarifies that cleanliness, order, and beauty are important but also "indifferent": "And all this he doth, not as out of necessity, or as putting a holiness in the things, but as desiring to keep the middle way between superstition, and slovenlinesse" (246). Significantly, Herbert also refers in this chapter to the "Communion Table", not an altar. "The Parson in Sacraments" requires the minister's deepest reverence, and the parishioners' kneeling at communion, but the chapter also calls it a "feast of Charity" rather than a sacrifice (257–9). "Old Customes" are respected by the Parson, but the Stuart "Book of Sports" never mentioned. Herbert does insist on the power of "The Parson Blessing" as a mark of the spiritual authority of the priesthood, but he is at pains to prove through argument and Biblical citation that the Apostles frequently used this mode of address. The most compelling chapter in this regard is "The Parson arguing", which portrays the ideal minister, or Herbert, courteously seeking out the "Papist" and the "Schismatick" in his community in order to talk them back into "the common Faith". As in *Musae Responsoriae* in 1620–1, so in *The Country Parson* in 1632, Herbert leads his sheep, "safest in a *via media*."[7]

Notes

Preface

1. Joseph Summers, *George Herbert* (Cambridge: Harvard University Press, 1968), 33, 35, 208. See also V.A. Rowe, "The Influence of the Earls of Pembroke on Parliamentary Elections, 1625–41." *English Historical Review* 50 (1935): 242–56.
2. Walton, *Lives* (London: Oxford University Press, 1966), 276; *The Works of George Herbert,* ed. F.E. Hutchinson (Oxford: Clarendon Press, 1941), xxx–xxxv; Amy Charles, *A Life of George Herbert* (Ithaca: Cornell University Press, 1977), 78–79,87–88.
3. Louis Martz, *The Poetry of Meditation* (New Haven: Yale University Press, 1954); Barbara Lewalski, *Protestant Poetics and the Seventeenth-Century Religious Lyric* (Princeton: Princeton University Press, 1979).
4. *The Norton Anthology of English Literature* (ed. M.H. Abrams, Stephen Greenblatt, 7th edition, [New York: Norton, 2000], 1:1218). See also note 39 in Chapter 5.
5. Cooley, "John Davenant, *The Country Parson*, and Herbert's Calvinist Conformity", *George Herbert Journal* 23:1&2 (Fall 1999-Spring 2000):8; Schoenfeldt, *Prayer and Power* (Chicago: University of Chicago Press, 1991), 36–37, 99; Jeffrey Powers-Beck, *Writing the Flesh* (Pittsburgh: Duquesne University Press, 1998); Malcolmson, *Heart-Work* (Stanford: Stanford University Press, 1999). On coteries, see Malcolmson, 46–68; and Greg Miller, "Scribal and Print Publication: The Case of George Herbert's English Poems", *The George Herbert Journal* 23:1&2 (Fall 1999–Spring 2000): 14–34. On common prayer, see Ramie Targoff *Common Prayer: The Language of Public Devotion in Early Modern England* (Chicago: University of Chicago Press, 2001). On public issues, see Sidney Gottlieb, "The Social and Political Backgrounds of George Herbert's Poetry", in *"The Muses Commonweale"*, ed. Claude Summers and Ted-Larry Pebworth (Columbia: University of Missouri, 1988), 107–18; Leah Marcus, *Childhood and Cultural Despair*, (Pittsburgh: University of Pittsburgh, 1978); Summers and Pebworth, "Public Concerns in Private Modes", *George Herbert Journal* 3:1&2 (1978/80): 1–21.
6. Charles, 185; Hutchinson, liii. In the passages quoted by Doerksen from exchange of letters between Nicholas and Arthur Woodnoth before the publication of Herbert's poems, the phrase *The Temple* is never used. See "Nicholas Ferrar, Arthur Woodnoth, and the Publication of George Herbert's *The Temple*, 1633", *George Herbert Journal* 3: 1&2 (1979–80): 23–4.

7. Hutchinson, liii; Annabel M. Endicott, "The Structure of George Herbert's *Temple*: A Reconsideration", *UTQ* 34 (1965), 226–237.
8. Doerksen, "'Too Good for Those Times': Politics and the Publication of George Herbert's *The Country Parson*", *Seventeenth-Century News*, (Spring/Summer 1991), 10–13.
9. Charles, 218-223.
10. The "B" manuscript was a fair copy made for the licensers by those at Little Gidding apparently from the original given them by Herbert. On the manuscripts, see Hutchinson, l–liv, lxxii–lxxiii; Charles, 182, n.11.
11. For their help on this volume, I would especially like to thank Paula Kennedy of Palgrave, U.K., Shirley Tan of Expo Holdings, and Matteo Pangallo, who provided the index.

Chapter 1   The Sidney-Herbert Coterie

1. Arthur Marotti, *John Donne: Coterie Poet* (Madison: University of Wisconsin Press, 1986); Harold Love, *Scribal Publication in Seventeenth-Century England* (Oxford: Clarendon Press, 1993). See also E.F. Hart, "The Answer-Poem of the Early Seventeenth-Century", *Review of English Studies* n.s., 7 (1956): 19–29; and J.W. Saunders, *The Profession of English Letters* (London: Routledge and Kegan Paul, 1964).
2. Pebworth, "John Donne, Coterie Poetry, and the Text as Performance", *Studies in English Literature* 49 (Winter 1989): 61–75; Philip J. Finkelpearl, *John Marston of the Middle Temple* (Cambridge: Harvard University Press, 1969).
3. (London: Matthew Inman, 1660).
4. "'Your Vertuous and Learned Aunt': The Countess of Pembroke as a Mentor to Mary Wroth," in *Reading Mary Wroth: Representing Alternatives in Early Modern England*, eds. Naomi J. Miller, Gary Waller (Knoxville: University of Tennessee Press, 1991), 16–34. Josephine Roberts points out that the last sonnet in Wroth's sequence *Pamphilia* to *Amphilanthus* turns to divine love (*The Poems of Mary Wroth* [Batan Range: Louisiana State University Press, 1983], 49).
5. Hart, "The Answer-Poem".
6. 38–9.
7. Martz developed the term "sacred parody" in *Poetry of Meditation*, 186.
8. *Works*, ed. Hutchinson. All subsequent references to Herbert's works quote from this edition, and will at times be signaled by page numbers.
9. *Philip Sidney*, ed. Katherine Duncan-Jones (Oxford: Oxford University Press, 1989), 246, 215. All other references to Sidney's work quote from this edition.
10. Burning was not the normal death for the early Christian martyrs, but it was for English heretics. "Showls" however is a reference to the symbol of the fish used by early Christians.

11. "Certayne notes of Instruction concerning the making of verse or ryme in English", *Works*, ed. John W. Cunliffe, 2 vols. (London: Cambridge University Press, 1907) I:465–6.

12. *Faerie Queene*, Book I, canto 2, stanzas : 40–41. See also Nancy Vickers, "Diana Described: Scattered Women and Scattered Rhyme" in *Writing and Sexual Difference*, ed. Elizabeth Abel (Chicago: University of Chicago Press, 1982), 95–109.

13. *The Poems English and Latin of Edward Lord Herbert of Cherbury*, ed. G.C. Moore Smith (Oxford: Clarendon Press, 1968), 51.

14. *William Shakespeare: The Complete Works*, ed. Alfred Harbage (Baltimore: Penguin Books, 1969), 5.1.180–2.

15. *Poems Written by the Right Honorable William Earl of Pembroke*, 9.

16. *The Countess of Pembroke's Arcadia*, a facsimile of the 1590 edition (Kent State University Press, 1970), 1:52, 55.

17. *Poems Written by the Right Honorable William Earl of Pembroke*, 19.

18. *The Countess of Pembroke's Arcadia*, 51–7. *Sidney*, 215.

19. *England's Helicon 1600, 1614* ed. Hyder Edward Rollins 2 vols. (Cambridge: Harvard University Press, 1935), 1:1.

20. Quoted from *Prosopopeia (1596)* in John Tobin, *George Herbert: Complete English Poems*, (London: Penguin Books, 1991), 351.

21. *Shakespeare's Sonnets*, ed. Katherine Duncan-Jones (Thomas Nelson & Sons Ltd.: Croatia, 1997), 21.

22. *William Shakespeare: The Complete Works*, xv.

23. *Shakespeare's Sonnets*, 52–71.

24. Fram Dinshaw, "A Lost MS of George Herbert's Occasional Verse and the Authorship of 'To the L. Chancellor'", *N&Q* 30 (October 1983), pp. 423–5. Hutchinson, 209, 437, 551, 597–8.

25. Edward Herbert, *Poems*, 34–8, 60, 97. See Kim Hall's discussion of the poems by Edward and George in *Things of Darkness; Economies of Race and Gender in Early Modern England* (Ithaca: Cornell University Press, 1995).

26. *Poems Written by the Right Honorable William Earl of Pembroke*, 93.

27. Joel Altman, *The Tudor Play of Mind: Rhetorical Inquiry and the Development of Elizabethan Drama (Berkeley: University of California Press, 1978)*.

28. Edward Herbert, *Poems*, 35.

29. *The Latin Poetry of George Herbert*, ed. Mark McCloskey and Paul R. Murphy (Athens: Ohio State University Press, 1965), 170–1.

30. See Schoenfeldt's fascinating discussion of sexuality and courtiership in the poem, 234–7.

31. Chambers thinks "Soules Joy" is by Donne, but Grierson, Summers, and Tuve conclude that the poem is by William Herbert. It is assigned to William in the 1660 edition of *Poems* by William Herbert and Rudyerd edited by John Donne's son and in Lansdowne MS 777. It is assigned to Donne in *1635–69* and the O'Flaherty manuscript. Summers' attribution of the poem to Pembroke is found in *George Herbert: His Religion and Art* (Cambridge, Mass.: Harvard University Press, 1968), 205. "Absence" is

attributed by most editors to John Hoskyns. It is attributed to Donne in a 1711 collection (see Grierson, II.cl). There is a very slight chance that Donne wrote "Absence", "Soules Joy", and "Valediction: forbidding Mourning", in which case Herbert's "Parodie" would be an answer primarily to Donne. But this set of poems is also related to Edward Herbert's "I must depart", Sidney's "Oft have I mused", and the four other absence poems in *A Poetical Rhapsody*. Doubters should consider that there are limits to the virtue of skepticism. On the views of Chambers and Grierson, see *The Poems of John Donne*, ed. Herbert J.C. Grierson, 2 vols. (London: Oxford University Press, 1912), 1:cxxxv–cxxxvi; see also Tuve, "Sacred 'Parody' of Love Poetry and Herbert" in *Essays by Rosemond Tuve*, ed. Thomas R. Roche, Jr. (Princeton: Princeton University Press, 1970).

32. *John Donne: The Elegies and the Songs and Sonnets*, ed. Helen Gardner (Oxford: Clarendon Press, 1965), 62–63.

33. "Absence" was first printed in *A Poetical Rhapsody*, edited by Francis Davison, published in 1602, and frequently reprinted. According to Michael Brennan, "His edition was regarded by those familiar with the ways of the court as a bold attempt to use literature to attract the interest of influential patrons" (*Literature and Patronage in the English Renaissance: The Pembroke Family* [London: Routledge, 1988], 1. The miscellany is dedicated to William Herbert, newly made earl of Pembroke, and includes poems by Philip Sidney and his sister Mary Sidney Herbert. It is likely that George Herbert knew this volume well, not only because it was also published in 1608, 1611, and 1621, but also because it includes a secular love poem patterned in the shape of an altar, and thought to be one of Herbert's models for his own poem "The Altar". It is instructive that *A Poetical Rhapsody* also includes four other poems on absence, six invectives against love or women, and, surprisingly enough, five religious poems.

34. Edward Herbert, 17; see also 19. Edward Herbert's "Ode upon a Question Moved" and Donne's "Exstasie" develop the topic of mutual love as well. Both poems may be responses to Sidney's Eighth Song in *Astrophil and Stella*. In the Eighth Song, Sidney writes that Astrophel and Stella, "while their eyes by love directed,/ Interchangeably reflected" meet for "mutual comfort" (6; 15–16). In his "Ode", Edward Herbert writes of "our equal loves", "that mutually happy pair", "each shall be both, yet both but one" (*Poems*, 61–66). Sir Herbert Grierson and Eugene Hill claim that Herbert's "Ode upon a Question Moved" responded to Donne's poem; Gardner suggests they were "rival rehandlings" of Sidney's dialogue of lovers, the Eighth Song. Grierson, ed. *The Poems of John Donne* (Oxford: Oxford University Press, 1912), 2:14. Eugene Hill, *Edward Herbert, Lord Herbert of Cherbury* (Boston: G.K. Hall, 1987), 95–103. Gardner, *John Donne*, 256.

35. Grierson quotes William Herbert, 1:429–30.

36. Tuve, "Sacred 'Parody'", 236–7.

37. Herbert may have learned this technique from Wroth's answer to Donne, "Sweetest Love," published in 1621 (*Poems*, ed. Roberts, 100).

38. Tuve, "Sacred 'Parody'", 241–2.
39. See Helen Wilcox ("Herbert's Musical Contexts: From Countrey-Aires to Angels Musick", in *Like Season'd Timber*, ed. Edmund Miller and Robert DiYanni [New York: Peter Lang, 1987]) for evidence that Herbert set his poems to music and performed them before others.
40. Sir Philip Sidney *The Countess of Pembroke's Arcadia (The Old Arcadia)*, ed. Katherine Duncan-Jones (Oxford: Oxford University Press 1985), 94. William's poem is quoted in Gary Waller, *The Sidney Family Romance* (Detroit: Wayne State University Press, 1993), 177–8.
41. Quilligan, "Completing the Conversation", in *Shakespeare Studies* XXV, ed. Leeds Barroll (London: Associated University Presses, 1997), 42–49; Pritchard, "George Herbert and Lady Mary Wroth: A Root for 'The Flower'?" *Review of English Studies* n.s. 47:187 (1996): 386–9.

Chapter 2   Cambridge and University Works

1. He included the "Church-militant" in the later manuscript of *The Temple*, whereas *Passio Discerpta* and *Lucus* were removed.
2. Daniel W. Doerksen, *Conforming to the Word: Herbert, Donne, and the English Church before Laud* (Lewisburg: Bucknell University Press, 1997), 61ff.
3. Charles, 50–4; 71–2, 94–100.
4. *Epicedium Cantabrigiense, In obitum immaturum Henrici, Principis Walliae.* Cantabrigiae, Ex officina Cantrelli Legge, 1612.
5. *Donne's Poetical Works*, ed. H.J.C. Grierson, (Oxford: Oxford University Press, 1912), 267. For Beaulieu and Holles, see Roy Strong, *Henry, Prince of Wales* (New York: Thames and Hudson, 1986), 8, 225.
6. *The Latin Poetry of George Herbert*, trans. Mark McCloskey and Paul R. Murphy (Athens, Ohio: Ohio University Press, 1965), 159. All other citations to this poem refer to this edition. Translations are those of McCloskey and Murphy unless otherwise noted.
7. Virgil, *Ecloques, Georgics, Aenerd I-VI*, trans. H. Rushton Fairclough; rev. G.P. Goold (Cambridge: Harvard University Press, 1999), 262–263.
8. Translation of Delores M. O'Higgins. Thanks to her for advice on translation in Chapters 2 and 4.
9. My translation.
10. My translation.
11. If "iustus" is translated "impartial" as McCloskey and Murphy do, the poem may refer to James's favoritism toward the Scots and particularly the current royal favorite Robert Carr, made Viscount Rochester in 1611.
12. *Divine Poems*, ed. Helen Gardner (Oxford: Clarendon University Press, 1952), 52–53. Other citations to the poem refer to this edition.
13. McCloskey, 174–5.
14. Notes of Ben Jonson's *Conversations with William Drummond of Hawthornden* (London: Shakespeare Society, 1842), 8.
15. Gardner, 111–113, 138–147. See also David Novarr, *The Disinterred Muse: Donne's Texts and Contexts* (Ithaca: Cornell University Press, 1980), 103–7.

16. Hodgkins, 20. Kenneth Fincham identifies "conformist Calvinist" as one of four possible positions within the Church of England during James I's reign, *Early Stuart Church, 1603–1642* (Stanford: Stanford University Press, 1993), 6–10.

17. Hutchinson, 588; Charles, 91; W. Hilton Kelliher, "The Latin Poetry of George Herbert", *The Latin Poetry of English Poets* ed. J.W. Binn (London: Routledge & Kegan Paul, 1974), 27.

18. Walton, 272–3 .

19. Novarr, *The Making of Walton's Lives,* 347–8, Walton, 270–1.

20. McCloskey, p. 3, "To James", lines 4–5. Further citations to *Musae Responsoriae* will refer to this edition.

21. "The Contexts of George Herbert's *Musae Responsoriae*", *George Herbert Journal* 15:3 (Spring 1992): 42–51. See also Kelliher, 27–8.

22. For the translation, see *The Complete Works in Verse and Prose of George Herbert*, ed. Rev. Alexander Grosart, (Fuller Worthies Library: London: Robson's and Sons, 1874) 3: 466–472.

23. Nicholas Tyacke, *Anti-Calvinists* (Oxford: Clarendon, 1987), 42.

24. Tyacke, 45.

25. *The Early Stuart Church,* 1–22.

26. Hodgkins, 20.

27. Kenneth Alan Hovey, "George Herbert's Authorship of 'To the Queene of Bohemia'", *Renaissance Quarterly* 30:1 (Spring 1977): 43–50; Ted-Larry Pebworth, "George Herbert's Poems to the Queen of Bohemia: A Rediscovered Text and a New Edition", in *English Literary Renaissance* 1:1 (Winter 1979): 108–120.

28. Leicester Bradner has demonstrated that Herbert wrote two short congratulatory verses to the couple on their marriage in 1613, which were included in a Cambridge volume presented to Frederick ("New Poems by George Herbert: The Cambridge Latin Gratulatory Anthology of 1613", *Renaissance News* 15 (1962): 208–11). Herbert would also have been well informed of events on the continent through his brother Edward, who visited the couple at least twice, through John Donne, who preached before them in Prague, and through Francis Nethersole, who became Lady Elizabeth's secretary in 1619 after handing over to deputy orator Herbert his duties as Public Orator of Cambridge (see Hovey, 45–6). There is in fact evidence that Herbert and Nethersole corresponded with each other (Hutchinson, Letter #VII, 369). Ted-Larry Pebworth has found a manuscript associated with Cambridge that he believes provides a better text. The manuscript attributes to a "G.H." the consolatory poems to Lady Elizabeth, and uses the title quoted above.

29. I quote from Pebworth's edition. See also Hutchinson, 211–213.

30. Hutchinson, 456; trans. Grosart, 433–4.

31. Grosart, 449.

32. *The Thirty Years' War*, ed. Geoffrey Parker (London: Routledge, 1997), 42–63.

33. Grosart, 449.

34. Parker, 56–8.

35. Fincham, *Stuart Church*, 34–35
36. *True Copies ... With Their Translations into English*. (London: W. Stansby for Richard Meighen, 1623), A3.
37. Thomas Baker, "The Reception of K. James, the Prince, the Palsgrave at Cambridge ...", British Library Harley MS. 7041, f. 38v–39. Thanks to Rachel Stockdale of the British Library for her help on this.
38. Grosart, 442. For Mede's comments, see his letters in British Library Harley MS. 389, f. 292. For Dr. Beale's oration, see *True Copies*, A4v.
39. Daniel J. Vitkus, "Trafficking with the Turk: English Travelers in the Ottoman Empire during the early Seventeenth-Century", in *Travel Knowledge*, ed. Ivo Kamps and Jyotsna G. Singh (New York: Palgrave, 2001), 48.
40. Palmer, 61.
41. Hutchinson, 601; Joseph Summers, *George Herbert: His Religion and Art* (Cambridge: Harvard University Press, 1968), 40–43; Charles, 100.
42. "Conquering Laurels and Creeping Ivy: The Tangled Politics of Herbert's *Reditum Caroli*", *George Herbert Journal* 17 (fall 1993): 14.
43. B.L Harl. MS. 389, f. 366 on 11 October 1623.
44. Roger Lockyer, *Buckingham* (London: Longman, 1981), 169–74.
45. Malcolmson, 21. On Pembroke's influence over the election to the seat that Herbert held, see V.A. Rowe, "The Influence of the Earls of Pembroke on Parliamentary Elections, 1625–41", *English Historical Review* 50 (1935): 242–56. Joseph Summers comments that Herbert's election was "almost certainly" the work of the Earl, and that Herbert's brother Henry took the same seat in 1626 (33; 208, note 24).
46. Grosart, 403–405. Page numbers to this edition will appear after subsequent citations.
47. *The Latin Poetry of English Poets*, pp. 34–45.
48. McCloskey, 164–5.
49. McCloskey, 97.
50. Kelliher, 39–40.
51. Kelliher, 43–45
52. McCloskey, 103.

Chapter 3   1624 and *The Temple*

1. There is some evidence that 1624 figured prominently in the construction of *The Temple*. Thomas Adams gave a sermon in August of that year called *The Temple*, and several issues in Adams' sermon are echoed in Herbert's work. *Passio Discerpta* and *Lucus*, linked with Herbert's University works, could not have been completed until after August 1623, and they were included with *The Temple* in its earliest manuscript form. They also use several themes important to *The Temple's* devotional lyrics, for example, a focus on the events of the passion as well as the hard heart transformed into an altar. The two collections of Latin epigrams also include poems specifically

associated with Herbert's role as apologist for the established church that he adopted when serving as Public Orator, for instance, his poetic exchange with Pope Urban VIII and his poem against war. This suggests that the manuscript, conventionally known as "W", coalesced after 1623. It may also have been conceived and planned as a work that, when published after Herbert's death, would associate him with the position of the Public Orator of Cambridge. Herbert did not resign from this position until after the death of his mother in 1627. *Passio Discerpta* and *Lucus* do not appear in the 1633 published edition or the "B" manuscript associated with it. This suggests that Herbert changed his mind about linking *The Temple* with these collections and the position of Public Orator after he resigned from that position in 1628. Therefore the "W" manuscript may have taken shape as a whole between the years 1624 and 1628.

2. Thanks to Sister Teresa of the Community of Saint Andrew and Neil Thomson, Secretary of the Diaconal Association of the Church of England, for their help on this.

3. Benet, "Herbert's Experience of Politics and Patronage in 1624", *George Herbert Journal* 10: 1&2 (1986/87): 44; Walton, 276; Charles, 112–113.

4. Novarr, *Walton's Lives*, 517; "*Review: A Life of George Herbert by Amy Charles*, 59–60.

5. Roger Lockyer, *Buckingham* (Longman: London, 1981), 180–217; Robert Ruigh, *The Parliament of 1624* (Cambridge: Harvard University Press, 1971), 149–256. On Buckingham and the privy councilors, particularly Pembroke, see Lockyer, 209, and Simon Adams, "Foreign Policy and the Parliaments of 1621 and 1624", and Kevin Sharpe, "The Earl of Arundel, His Circle and the Opposition to the Duke of Buckingham, 1618–1628", in *Faction and Parliament*, ed. Kevin Sharpe (Oxford:Oxford University Press, 1978), 159, 226–7.

6. Ruigh, 211. The Michaelmas session was prorogued on October 1, 1624, until February 26, 1625, delayed again in January, but never held because of the death of King James on March 27 (Charles, 113).

7. Lockyer, 276, 305, 321–331; Sharpe, "The Earl of Arundel", 228. See also Richard Cust, *The Forced Loan* (Oxford: Clarendon Press, 1987), 23–27.

8. Charles, 106–7.

9. Charles, 107–9; A.L. Maycock, *Nicholas Ferrar of Little Gidding* (London: Society for Promotion of Christian Knowledge, 1938), 23.

10. Schoenfeldt, "Submission and Assertion: The 'Double Motion' of Herbert's 'Dedication'", *John Donne Journal* 2:2 (1983): 39–49; "'Respective Boldness': Herbert and the Art of Submission", in *A Fine Tuning*, ed. Mary Maleski (Binghamton, N.Y.: Medieval and Renaissance Texts and Studies, 1989) , 79–94.

11. In a letter printed in the 1633 edition, Nicholas Ferrar emphasizes the significance of this poem: "The dedication of this work having been made by the Authour to the *Divine Majestie* onely, how should we now

presume to interest any mortall man in the patronage of it?" (3). For a discussion of Ferrar's reasons for stating this, see Daniel W. Doerksen, "Nicholas Ferrar, Arthur Woodnoth, and the Publication of George Herbert's *The Temple*, 1633", *George Herbert Journal* 3: 1&2 (1979–80): 325–6.

12. My translation.

13. For a different view, see Guibbory, 51.

14. E. Cobham Brewer, *Dictionary of Phrase and Fable*. (London: Cassell and Company, Ltd., 1849).

15. Malcolmson, 2–15, 69–82.

16. Hutchinson suggests that Herbert wrote the work early and revised it often (476). Charles posits the date of 1614 for the composition of a major portion of the work, the same date she offers for Herbert's letter of advice to his brother Henry (78). Strier agrees it is an early work, and that the lyrics of "The Church" display Herbert's "revulsion" at the "prudential and self-enhancing considerations" of the earlier poem ("Sanctifying", 55). Debora Shuger reads "The Church-porch" as simultaneous with "The Church", and as representing the entirely separate realms of the public courtier and the private soul (93). Michael Schoenfeldt reads the precepts of "The Church-porch" not in contrast with but in order to illuminate the lyrics of "The Church". See a summary of other approaches to the poem and the structure of *The Temple* as a whole in Fish, *Living Temple*, 8–10.

17. See note 1 above, and Chapter 5 for information on the manuscripts.

18. Fish, *The Living Temple*, 125–131.

19. Doerksen finds *The Temple* more Calvinist than *Musae Responsoriae*. See *Conforming to the Word*, 85–8.

20. McCloskey, 106–7.

21. Tyacke, 117–8. See Kathleen Lynch, "George Herbert's Holy 'Altar': Name and Thing", *George Herbert Journal* 17:1 (Fall 1993): 41–60.

22. Conrad Russell, *Crisis of Parliaments* (London: Oxford University Press, 1971), 315; Tyacke, *Anti-Calvinists*, 199–216; Sharpe, *Personal Rule of Charles I*, 333–344; Tyacke, *Aspects of English Protestantism*, 194–5.

23. Fish, *Self-Consuming Artifacts*; 207–15. See Exodus 22:25 and Deut. 27:2–5.

24. Schoenfeldt, 161–7; Strier, 191–5; Targoff, 100–101.

25. Sonnets to his mother (206). This suggests that the meaning of the image of the altar changed for him over time from a reference to the "sacrifice" to God of his poetic powers to questions about liturgy and theology associated with Arminianism. The contrast between this poem and other formal altar poems either by love poets or those dedicating themselves to the king suggests other resonances for the poem (C.A. Patrides, *The English Poems of George Herbert* [London: Dent, 1974], 209; Malcolmson, 84–6).

26. *Book of Common Prayer*, (London: Oxford University Press), 316.

27. *Book of Common Prayer*, 313.

28. Ilona Bell, "'Setting Foot into Divinity': George Herbert and the English Reformation", *Essential Articles for the Study of George Herbert's Poetry* (Hamden, CT.: Archon Books, 1979), 63–83.

29. *George Herbert: The Complete English Poems* (London: Penguin, 1991), 335.

30. *Ploughshares* 2:4 (1975): 187–205.

31. Tyacke, *Anti-Calvinists*, 48–9, 102–3, 113–4, 164–79.

32. *Protestant Poetics and the Seventeenth-Century Religious Lyric* (Princeton: Princeton University Press, 1979), 289–90.

33. Ernest Lee Tuveson, *Millennium and Utopia* (New York: Harper and Row, 1964). 22–70.

34. Hutchinson, 543; Charles, 82; Hodgkins, 24, 106–7; Powers-Beck, 190–221, particularly 217–8.

35. Hodgkins, 186; Powers-Beck, 219.

36. "George Herbert's Authorship of 'To the Queene of Bohemia'", 48. See also Hovey, "'Wheeled about ... into *Amen*': 'The Church Militant' on Its Own Terms", *George Herbert Journal* 10: 1&2 (Fall 1986/Spring 1987).

37. Malcolmson, 179–204.

38. Hutchinson, 547.

39. Charles, 185; Hutchinson, liii.

40. Annabel M. Endicott, "The Structure of George Herbert's *Temple*: A Reconsideration", *UTQ* 34 (1965), 226–237.

41 "The Architectonics of George Herbert's *The Temple*", *ELH* 29 (1962): 289–305.

42. Endicott; Lee Ann Johnson, "The Relationship of 'The Church Militant' to *The Temple*", *SP* 67 (April 1971): 200–206; Lewalski, 288; Fish, *Living Temple*, 154.

43. Fish, *Living Temple*, 140, 145ff.

44. *Reformation Spirituality* (London: Associated University Presses, 1985) 228–243, particularly 229.

Chapter 4   1627 and Herbert's Mother

1. *A Sermon* of *commemoracon of the ladye Danvers by John Donne ... with other Commemoracions of her by George Herbert* (London: Philemon Stephens and Christopher Meredith, 1627), entered at Stationer's Hall, July 7. Donne's sermon was preached on July 1, in Chelsea. For evidence of his health problems, see *Works*, XXV, 363, 364, 372–4.

2. Summers writes, "Whatever Herbert's attitude, his unemployment was a material fact; from 1619 until 1630 there was no offer of employment from that Court to which he looked" (39).

3. Malcolmson, 15–25. The experience of Herbert's brothers is telling in this regard. Buckingham appointed Edward Herbert as ambassador to France in 1619, but this was significantly before the conflict between Pembroke and Buckingham developed fully. Henry Herbert obtained his position as Master of the Revels through the influence of Pembroke, but

King James granted it to him in 1623, and after some question over rights to the position by one of Buckingham's clients. After tensions between Pembroke and Buckingham became strong, in 1625 and, especially 1626, when Pembroke's clients led the battle for Buckingham's impeachment, Edward Herbert received very little from the court in payment or patronage. Thomas Herbert served as captain to the ship that brought Charles and Buckingham back from Spain in 1623, and Buckingham named him as captain to the Dreadnought in the expedition to Cadiz in 1625. However, after the failure of that mission, Thomas received nothing else from the court. Both Edward and Thomas protested at the court's negligence in promoting them. I believe that George did the same, but in more indirect ways. See Lockyer, 176–6, 276; Richard Cust, *The Forced Loan and English Politics, 1626–1628* (Oxford: Clarendon Press, 1987) 23–7. On Thomas, see *The Autobiography of Edward Lord Herbert of Cherbury* (London: Alexander Murray, 1870), 19. On Edward, see *DNB*.

4. Fincham, *Early Stuart Church* and *Prelate as Pastor*; Tyacke, *Anti-Calvinists*, 166–7. Kevin Sharpe argues against Tyacke in *The Personal Rule of Charles I* (New Haven: Yale University Press, 1992) 275–402; Tyacke responds in *Aspects of English Protestantism c.1530–1700* (Manchester: Manchester University Press, 2001),176–202.

5. Quoted in R.C. Bald, *John Donne: A Life* (Oxford: Clarendon Press, 1970), 276.

6. Walton, 276–7.

7. On the oration of 1626 and the installation at Lincoln, see Charles, 121–124. On the Bacon collection, see Hutchinson, xxx,599.

8. Summers, 33, 208; Lockyer, 176–7, 276, 332–3; Cust, *The Forced Loan,* 23–7.

9. Tyacke, 48–9, 113–4, 164–79.

10. On Pembroke as patron to Herbert, see Chapter 5, page 6. Also, see Summers, 33, 35, 208.

11. Charles, 134–5.

12. See Hutchinson, 470; Grosart, 473–477. The letter is dated May 6 but gives no year. In 1625, Herbert Thorndike served as deputy orator. The letter could not have been written in 1626, since it is dated May, and Herbert seems quite ready to perform his duties in July of that year. It also could not have been written in 1628, since Herbert had already resigned by January.

13. Hutchinson, xxx, 599.

14. McCloskey, 172–3.

15. For Philomela, see Ovid, *Metamorphosis* VI.425–721; for Flora, *Fasti* V. 195ff.

16. Bacon's *Great Instauration* was never finished. Hutchinson (599) described a 1813 printing of the volume in memory of Bacon, which includes a note referring to Herbert's copy of the volume published in 1626 (now lost), in which he has transcribed two dedications from Thomas Peyton's *Glasse of Time* (1620 and 1623). Peyton's dedication to Bacon defends his impartial justice and lack of interest in money. The

dedication to Charles urges him to follow the example of his father, and predicts his worth will be sounded "as farre as India lies" (*Glasse of Time*, [New York: John R. Alder, 1886], xxxiv–xxxvi).

17. See Schoenfeldt's fascinating discussion of this poem (234–7). Fram Dinshaw defends Herbert's authorship of these poems in "A Lost MS. Of George Herbert's Occasional Verse" and the Authorship of "To the Lord Chancellor", *Notes and Queries* 30 (October 1983): 423–425.

18. Charles, 78; Hutchinson, xl, 480; Aubrey, *Brief Lives*, ed. Oliver Dick (Ann Arbor: University of Michigan Press, 1957), 9.

19. *Advancement*,ed. G.W. Kitchin (London: Dent, 1973), 142.

20. *The Proficience and Advancement of Learning* in *Francis Bacon: A Selection of His Works*, ed. Sidney Warhaft (New York: The Odyssey Press, 1965), 223.

21. McCloskey, 168–171.

22. Warhaft, 313.

23. Grosart, 436–7.

24. Kelliher, 46.

25. *The Translation of Certaine Psalmes into English Verse* (London: Barret and Whitaker, 1625), A3.

26. Kelliher, 48.

27. Pearlman, "Herbert's God," *English Literary Renaissance* 13 (Winter 1983), 90, 109.

28. McCloskey, 121.

29. "The Mourner in the Flesh: George Herbert's Commemoration of Magdalen Herbert in *Memoriae Matris Sacrum*" in *Men Writing the Feminine: Literature, Theory, and the Question of Genders*, ed. Thais E. Morgan (Albany: State University of New York Press, 1994), 15.

30. Rubin, "Let your death be my *Iliad*": Classic Allusion and Latin in George Herbert's *Memoriae Matris Sacrum*" in *Reconsidering the Renaissance*, ed. Mario A. De Cesare (Binghamton: Center for Medieval and Early Renaissance Studies, 1992), 438–9.

31. Rubin "Mourner" 27, note 18.

32. Pearlman, 96; Rubin, 21.

33. Pearlman, 92, Rubin, "Mourner," 19, 23.

34. My translation.

35. McCloskey, 152–153.

36. Lockyer, 378.

37. Palmer, xxxi, 69–70.

38. McCloskey, 149–143; my translation.

39. Kelliher, 53.

40. My translation.

41. Kelliher, 48.

42. Kelliher, 48.

43. Kelliher, 47.

44. McCloskey, 154–5.

Chapter 5 *The Temple*: Poems on Grace, Employment, and the Church

1. Walton, 276–288; Charles, 145–7; Cooley, 8; Schoenfeldt, 36–37, 99.
2. Malcolmson, 9–11, 96–204.
3. Tyacke, *Anti-Calvinists*, 162.
4. Cooley, 8; Fincham, *Early Stuart Church*, 37–8, 85.
5. Herbert comments on the ambition of the clergy as a "common temptation" in *The Country Parson*, 238.
6. On "W" and "B" manuscripts, see Hutchinson, l–liv. The "B" manuscript was a fair copy made for the licensers by those at Little Gidding apparently from the original given them by Herbert. See Hutchinson, lxxii–lxxiii; Charles, 182, n. 11. See notes below for information about dating the manuscripts.
7. See Joseph Summers, "whatever Herbert's attitude, his unemployment was a material fact: from 1619 until 1630 there was no offer of employment from that Court to which he looked" (39).
8. Doerksen, *Conforming to the Word;*, Fish, *Self-Consuming Artifacts;* Halewood, Hodgkins, Strier, Veith.
9. Tyacke, *Anti-Calvinists*, 48–9, 102–3, 113–4, 164–79.
10. Cooley, 6.
11. Achsah Guibbory argues in her fascinating and useful volume that Herbert brings into a difficult tension the two cultures of the English Reformation that would pull apart in the English Civil War: ceremonialism and individual devotion (*Ceremony and Community from Herbert to Milton* (Cambridge: Cambridge University Press, 1998), 44–78. But Guibbory does not acknowledge the category "conforming Calvinist" used by historians like Tyacke and Fincham (as well as literary critics like Doerksen) to represent such a combination throughout the reign of James I and after. See Hodgkins on "the middle way".
12. Cooley, 6; Kevin Sharpe, *The Personal Rule of Charles I* (New Haven, Yale University Press, 1992), 345–8; Tyacke, *Aspects of English Protestantism*, 195.
13. Horton Davies, *Worship and Theology in England* (Princeton: Princeton University Press, 1975), 2:39.
14. Charles, 135–7, 141–5.
15. Walton, 284–5; Hutchinson, xxxiii.
16. *DNB*.
17. Walton, 286; Charles, 144; David Novarr, "Review: *A Life of George Herbert* by Amy Charles", *George Herbert Journal* 1:2 (1978): 56, 62.
18. Hutchinson, xxxi.
19. Charles, 136–7.
20. Malcolmson, 179–204.
21. Charles, 145–153.
22. Charles, 145; Hutchinson, xxxiv–v; Walton, 287.
23. Novarr, "Review", 55–6.

24. *Handbook of British Chronology*, ed. E.B. Fryde, D.E. Greenway, S. Porter, 3rd edition (London: Offices of the Royal Historical Society, 1986), 226. Thanks to Gabriel Linehan of the Lambeth Palace Library for this information.
25. Tyacke, *Anti-Calvinists*, 79–80.
26. Charles, 154.
27. Hutchinson, xxxix.
28. Daniel W. Doerksen, "Nicholas Ferrar, Arthur Woodnoth, and the Publication of George Herbert's *The Temple*, 1633", *George Herbert Journal* 3: 1&2 (1979–80): 325–6.
29. Charles, 135.
30. Charles, 135, 154.
31. Hutchinson, xxxvi.
32. Tuve, "Sacred Parody".
33. Cooley, 1–7.
34. Novarr, "Review", 54.
35. *DNB*.
36. Sharpe, *Personal Rule*, 63–104.
37. Richard D. Braun and Jack Tager, *Massachusetts: A Concise History* (Amherst: University of Massachusetts Press, 2000), 11–35; Robert C. Winthrop, *Life and Letters of John Winthrop*, 2 vols., (Boston: Little, Braun, 1869), I:309–11.
38. Walton, 315; Hutchinson, 546–7. Hutchinson suggests that many shared Herbert's views, and provides examples from 1634 and 1725, evidence that undermines the claim that "The Church-militant" must be an early poem.
39. Walton, 307–15; Novarr, *The Making of Walton's Lives*, 323–7. J. Max Patrick does not accept the truth of any aspect of Walton's story ["The Editor as Critic", The William Clark Memorial Library, University of California, Los Angeles, 1973). I quote Walton's account of Herbert's speech: "*Sir, I pray deliver this little Book to my dear brother Farrer, and tell him, he shall find in it a picture of the many spiritual Conflicts that have past betwixt God and my Soul, before I could subject mine to the will of Jesus, my Master: in whose service I have now found perfect freedom; desire him to read it: and then, if he can think it may turn to the advantage of any dejected poor Soul, let it be made publick: if not, let him burn it: for I and it, are less than the least of God's mercies*" (314). The influence of Walton's account is so great that the *Norton Anthology of English Literature* reports this speech as "Herbert's own description of the collection" (ed. M.H. Abrams, Stephen Greenblatt, 7th Edition, [New York: Norton, 2000] 1:1595), and adds as well that Herbert destroyed his English secular lyrics, although there is absolutely no evidence of this whatsoever (1:1218).
40. See Guibbory, 44–78.
41. See Tyacke, 48–9, 113–4, 164–79. The parson preaching chooses "texts of Devotion, not Controversie" (233). See also "Divinitie".
42. On Charles' proclamation, see Sharpe, 318–9.
43. It is significant that, even in *Musae Responsoriae*, controversy never centers on theology, but on conformity. See also "The Parson arguing": "whether

things once indifferent, being made by the precept of Authority more then indifferent, it be in our power to omit or refuse them" (263).

44. Stanley Fish, *Self-Consuming Artifacts* (Berkeley: University of California Press, 1972), 174–176.

45 Louis L. Martz argues that the poem allows for merit in "The Generous Ambiguity of George Herbert's *Temple* " in *A Fine Tuning*, ed. Mary Maleski (Binghamton, N.Y.: Medieval and Renaissance Texts and Studies, 1989), 31–56. Hodgkins refutes this view, 16–21.

46. Quoted in "Herbert's 'The Water-course': Notorious and Neglected", *Notes and Queries* 34 (1987): 311.

47. Malcolmson, 145–204.

48. 290.

49. 176–179.

50. The "W" manuscript included such an image for stanza 3 as well. See Hutchinson, p.89.

51. The devotional poetry in *Passio Discerpta* and *Lucus* have been dated around 1624; "In Natales et Pascha Concurrentes" has been dated as early as 1618. See Hutchinson, 591, 596.

52. See Doerksen, "Nicholas Ferrar".

53. On the "W" and "B" manuscripts, see note 6 above.

54. Charles argues that this period of unemployment occurred before Herbert became a deacon in 1624. I believe it occurred between 1624 and 1630, when Herbert became a priest (78–87). Therefore I also disagree with Charles about the dating of the "W" manuscript, which she sees as "the work of a layman", thus placing it before 1624 (81), whereas I date the manuscript to around 1627. See note #24, and Chapter 3, note #1.

55. See "The Flower".

56. See the poem's original ending in the "W" manuscript in Hutchinson, 57.

57. Charles dates "Affliction" (I) around 1617 (84–87). But it is difficult to imagine that the sense of anxiety expressed in the poem could refer to Herbert's career before 1624, given his rather remarkable string of achievements in the university and his seat in Parliament (see Chronology).

58. The image of the tree also appears in *Memoriae Matris Sacrum*, #11. I have argued in *Heart-Work* that this Latin poem and "Affliction" (I) have several similarities, and that "Affliction" (I) was written after the death of Herbert's mother (100–106). Because "Affliction" (I) appears in "W", I date the manuscript that eventually appeared as "B" as beginning after 1627.

59. Barnabas Oley, "A prefatory view of the life and virtues of the authour" (1671), printed in Grosart 3:225.

60. Gen. 32: 24–6; *OED*, I.2.c.

61. *OED* B.2.a,b.

62. Hodgkins, 127–141.

63. Schoenfeldt, 180–4.

64. According to the *OED*, "boards" did not refer to the stage of a theater until the mid-eighteenth century.

65. 127–47.
66. See the reference to "both Regiments" in "Frailtie", in which the word "brave" is also used to describe the upper-class life. Debora Shuger discusses the issue in *Habits of Thought in the English Renaissance* (Berkeley: University of California Press, 1990), 91–119.
67. Guibbory, 72.
68. Guibbory, 74, Hodgkins, 141–48, Strier, 127–33.
69. Hutchinson, 543.
70. Guibbory, 52–3.
71. "Magdalene Herbert: Towards a *Topos* for the Anglican Church", *George Herbert Journal* 1:2 (Spring 1978): 1–16.
72. *The Sermons of John Donne*, ed. Evelyn M. Simpson and George R. Potter, 10 vols. (Berkeley: University of California Press, 1962), vol. 8, 90.
73. McCloskey, 124–7.

Afterword: *The Country Parson*

1. "Nicholas Ferrar, Arthur Woodnoth, and the Publication of George Herbert's *The Temple*, 25–6.
2. Herbert wrote other prose works aside from *The Country Parson* during his years at Bemerton, including an English translation of a work by Luigi Cornaro, called *A Treatise of Temperance and Sobrietie, Brief Notes on Valdesso's Considerations* meant to accompany Nicholas Ferrar's translation, and a collection of *Outlandish Proverbs* (Hutchinson, 291–362). However *The Country Parson* provides the most insight into Herbert's attitude toward his work and his engagement in the world. The other works are interesting for a variety of reasons: Valdesso, for Herbert's views on theology; Cornaro, for his concerns about diet and the lifestyle of the landed elite. The proverbs have yet to receive serious attention, but should, since they probably have much to tell us about Herbert's interests and literary style.
3. A letter quoted by Doerksen demonstrates that Woodnoth and Sir John Danvers had access to *The Temple* after Herbert's death and before it was published (*Ibid*, 25).
4. "'Too Good for Those Times': Politics and the Publication of George Herbert's *The Country Parson*", *Seventeenth-Century News*, (Spring/Summer 1991), 10–13. Doerksen discusses the prayers on p. 11.
5. Malcolmson, 26–45; Veith, 228–250.
6. Cooley; Doerksen, *Conforming to the Word;* Hodgkins.
7. McCloskey, 59.

Index